NIKOLAI GOGOL

The Government Inspector

an English version by
EDWARD O. MARSH *and* JEREMY BROOKS

with commentary and notes by
NICK *and* NON WORRALL

METHUEN DRAMA

Methuen Drama Student Edition

10 9 8 7 6 5 4 3 2

This edition first published in the United Kingdom in 2003 by
Methuen Publishing Ltd

Methuen Drama
A & C Black Publishers Ltd
38 Soho Square, London WID 3HB

Reissued with additional material and a new cover design 2005

This translation of *The Government Inspector* first published in 1968 by
Methuen & Co. Ltd

Copyright © 1968 by Edward O. Marsh and Jeremy Brooks

Commentary and notes copyright © 2003, 2005 by Nick and Non
Worrall

The rights of the translators to be identified as the translators of these
works have been asserted by them in accordance with the Copyright,
Designs and Patents Act, 1988

A CIP catalogue record for this book is available from the
British Library

ISBN 9-780413-773210

Typeset by Deltatype Ltd, Birkenhead, Merseyside
Printed and bound in Great Britain by
Cox & Wyman Ltd, Reading, Berkshire

Contents

Nikolai Gogol: 1809–52

1809   Nikolai Vasilevich Gogol-Ianovski was born in the
Ukraine (Little Russia) in the town of Sorochintsy in
the province of Poltava, on 20 March. His father,
Vasili Afanasevich, who has connections with Polish
aristocracy (hence the Ianovski in his surname), owns
a small estate, Vasilevka, of 3000 acres with about 100
serfs. Vasili is also something of an amateur
playwright and the author of two comedies in
Ukrainian. Gogol himself is bilingual but writes only a
single epigram and one letter in Ukrainian during his
lifetime. He also drops the 'Ianovski' from his
surname. His mother, Maria Ivanovna Kosiarovskaia,
is devoted to her much older husband to whom she
bears twelve children, but only Gogol and three sisters
survive for any length of time. She is a lifelong
influence on her talented son of whom she is
especially proud even, in eccentric old age, attributing
to him the invention of the railway and the steamship.
Gogol never marries and, as far as is known, never has
sexual relations with a woman – a fact which
commentators attribute either to his idealism, his
neuroses, or his supposed homosexuality.

1818   Attends preparatory school in Poltava, central
−19   Ukraine.

1821   Attends the 'gimnazium' in Nezhin, a boarding
−28   school where he comes under the influence of some
good teachers and where he achieves success as an
actor in school plays, especially as a villainous Creon
in Ozerov's *Oedipus in Athens* and as the stupid
tyrannical despot, Madam Prostakova, who dotes on
her eponymous child in Fonvizin's *The Infant*. He
numbers among his school friends some who are also

going to make a name for themselves in the literary
world, including the playwright Nestor Kukolnik.
Gogol assists in producing and designing school
literary magazines with titles like *The Meteor of
Literature* and *Parnassian Dung*. He pens a satirical
comedy, *Something About Nezhin, or Fools Rush In
Where Angels Fear to Tread*. His schoolmates
nickname him 'the mysterious dwarf' but are fearful
of his sarcastic tongue. His first attempt at fiction is a
tale entitled 'The Brothers Tverdislavich', which is
criticised by a friend, Konstantin Bazili, so Gogol
burns it – initiating a self-destructive habit he is to
repeat.

1825 Death of his father on 31 March.

1828 Arrives in St Petersburg at the end of December, then
a city with a population of about 450,000, in company
with a school friend and neighbour, Aleksandr
Danilevsky, and seeks employment (successfully) in
the civil service and (unsuccessfully) in the theatre.
Subsequently, many of Gogol's acquaintances pay
tribute to his talents as an actor, especially when
reading his own plays.

1829 Publishes anonymously a short (five-stanza) poem,
'Italy', in the journal *Son of the Fatherland*. Another
long narrative poem or 'idyll in scenes', *Gants* [Hans]
Kiukhelgarten [Küchelgarten], is published at Gogol's
own expense (300 roubles; the poem retailed for five).
The work is a kind of hymn to art, beauty and the
glories of ancient Greece in the form of an aesthetic
pilgrimage. It is badly reviewed in the *Moscow
Telegraph* and *The Northern Bee* but otherwise ignored,
so Gogol requisitions all unsold copies of the book
and burns them before fleeing abroad to Lübeck, in
Germany. He returns to St Petersburg in September
and is heavily dependent on his mother's financial
support. In the same month he fails an audition at the
Aleksandrinsky Theatre, largely due to nerves.
In November he obtains a clerical post in the

Department of Government Properties and Public
Buildings on a salary of 30 roubles a month, where his
interest in architecture serves him well. He publishes
an article, 'On the Architecture of our Time', which
recommends the building of very high towers,
especially in capital cities. The highest salary he earns
as a civil servant is 750 roubles a year.

1830   Publishes anonymously in *Notes of the Fatherland* a
story, 'Bisavriuk, Or St John's Eve, told by the Sexton
of the Church of the Intercession', later included in
Evenings on a Farm Near Dikanka. Uses a variety of
pseudonyms for other articles. Transfers from his
government department to one at the Department for
Domains where he stays until February.

1831   Publishes an essay, 'Woman', which offers a
romantically idealised view of the sex. Begins to move
in St Petersburg literary circles and is introduced to
Pushkin in May.

1831   Employed as a teacher of history at the Patriotic
  –5   Institute for Girls on a salary of 400 roubles a year,
rising to 1200. Obtains educational places there for
two of his sisters.

1831   *Evenings on a Farm Near Dikanka* published under his
  –2   own name, although described as stories published by
a bee-keeper, Rudi [Ginger] Panko. The eight tales
are influenced by Ukrainian folklore and fairy tale and
feature the Devil, demons, sorcerers, ghosts, and
other supernatural entities.

1834   Appointed assistant professor of World History at St
Petersburg University. The future novelist Ivan
Turgenev is among his students. Gogol's knowledge
of medieval history seems to have been considerable
and he even contemplates writing a multi-volumed
(eight or nine) history of the Middle Ages as well as a
history of the Ukraine. However, after a promising
inaugural lecture in September, his powers as a
lecturer appear to decline to the point where his
students come to believe that he knows next to

nothing about his subject. According to Turgenev, Gogol sought to deflect criticism by appearing at his lectures with his head swathed in a black silk kerchief as if suffering from toothache, so as to avoid having to deliver the lectures himself.

1835   Quits his post at the university – 'Unappreciated I took the Chair, and unappreciated I leave it' – and virtually abandons his ambitions as a medieval historian, although an unfinished play, *Alfred*, based on the life of the cake-burning English king, shows his continuing interest in the subject. He also resigns from his post at the Patriotic Institute.

Publication of *Arabesques*, which consists of essays on many different subjects as well as the so-called 'Petersburg Tales' – 'The Portrait', a serious moral fable about a portrait which seems to come to life, with harrowing consequences for a money-obsessed artist; 'Nevski Prospekt', a story set on St Petersburg's main thoroughfare, which describes the fortunes in love of an idealistic artist and a philistine philanderer, the one ending in suicide, the other in comic humiliation; and 'Diary of a Madman', which takes the form of a diary written by a humble clerk with ambitions above his station, who falls for the boss's daughter, imagines he overhears conversations between her pet dog and another pooch, before, finally, coming to the conclusion that he is the King of Spain and ending up in a lunatic asylum.

Mirgorod also published, consisting of the rather sentimental 'Old-Fashioned Landowners'; 'Taras Bulba', a serious historical tale set among Ukrainian cossacks, 'The Viy' – a terrifying tale about the chief of gnomes whose eyelids droop to the ground, and a satirical grotesque 'Tale of how Ivan Ivanovich Quarrelled with Ivan Nikiforovich', which describes a petty quarrel between formerly friendly neighbours ending in litigation.

Around this time writes 'The Nose', a surreal story

about a major who wakes up one morning to find his
nose missing, only to encounter it in the street
masquerading as a civil servant with a rank higher
than his own. After a series of bizarre episodes, the
nose is restored to the major's face.

Begins work on his novel *Dead Souls*, in which the
central character, Chichikov, embarks on a
monumental swindle, whereby he purchases from
various landowners at a knockdown price dead
peasants whose names have not been removed from
the census and so, as far as officialdom is concerned,
are still 'alive'. This is in order to qualify for a
government grant which will allow him to settle these
'dead souls' (the words for 'soul', *dusha*, and 'peasant'
are synonymous in Russian) on an estate he will
purchase with the government money and where he
will live a life of luxury. Part One of the novel
concludes with the thwarting of Chichikov and his
departure from the town of 'N'. Part Two is proposed
as a positive moral rejoinder to the satirically negative
Part One but is never completed. A section survives
which is published as Part Two but most of it is
destroyed by Gogol himself.

In a fit of inspiration, having apparently acquired the
plot from Pushkin, Gogol completes *Revizor* (*The
Government Inspector/The Inspector General*) very
rapidly between November and December.

1836   First issue of the 'thick journal', *Sovremennik* [The
Contemporary], edited by Pushkin, on 11 April, in
which Gogol's story 'The Carriage' appears, as well as
'Morning of a Man of Affairs', the first act of an
uncompleted play *The Order of St Vladimir, Third
Class*, in which the rank-obsessed central character is
so intent on attaining the medal of St Vladimir that he
goes mad and imagines himself to be the insignia
itself. The journal also includes Gogol's article 'On
the literary-journalistic movement in 1834 and 1835'.
19 April. *The Government Inspector* is premièred at the

Aleksandrinsky Theatre in the presence of Tsar
Nicholas II and Gogol himself.

25 May. First performance in Moscow at the Maly
Theatre with the great 'Russian Garrick', Mikhail
Shchepkin, as the Mayor. Shchepkin, a fellow
Ukrainian, is later befriended by Gogol.

6 June. Confused and neurotically ambivalent about
the play's reception, Gogol flees abroad where he
spends most of the next twelve years – in Switzerland,
France and mainly in Italy where he becomes
especially attached to the city of Rome.

1836
–9

Lives abroad where he suffers intermittent bouts of
depression and hypochondria.

1836
–7

Spends the winter in Paris, where he writes a large
proportion of *Dead Souls* and sees productions at the
Comédie Française of plays by Molière and others.

1837

While in Rome, is distraught to learn of Pushkin's
death in a duel – the man to whom he claims he owes
everything as an artist. As he expresses it to his friend
Professor Mikhail Pogodin, 'I never undertook
anything, I never wrote anything without his advice. I
am indebted to him for all that is best in me.'

1838

Associates with expatriate Russian artists, such as
Aleksandr Ivanov, who uses Gogol as a model for
minor characters in his large canvas, *Christ's
Appearance Before the People*. He also seems to flirt
with the Catholic faith, while remaining loyal to the
Russian Orthodox Church, and establishes an intense
friendship with a young Russian aristocrat with a
terminal illness, Iosif Velgorski, who dies the
following year from tuberculosis. Gogol's short piece
'Nights in a Villa' refers to this episode.

1839
–40

Travels in France and Germany between September
and the following May when he returns to Russia.
Meets the radical critic Vissarion Belinski.

1840

Meets author of *Hero of our Time*, Mikhail Lermontov,
in May. Travels from Moscow to Rome with a friend,
Vasili Panov, before visiting Vienna and Venice and

returning to Rome via Florence.

1841 First part of *Dead Souls* completed in May. Despite its Russian milieu, most of the novel is composed abroad. The censors forbid publication in December.

1842 Lives abroad, mainly in Italy, while travelling
−8   extensively.

1842 His *Collected Works* published in four volumes.
−3

1844 Censor permits publication of *Dead Souls* in April. Gogol travels to Rome in May. Première of his play *Marriage* in St Petersburg on 9 September in which the central character, Podkolyosin, is persuaded into wooing one Agafya Tikhonovna in competition with other suitors, all of whom are uniquely grotesque. To his dismay, the reluctant Podkolyosin, having been press-ganged into proposing by his bullying friend, Kochkarev, succeeds in winning Agafya for himself. However, he manages to avoid the actual wedding, which has already been fixed, by escaping through a window.

A collection of Gogol's writings is published including, for the first time, 'The Overcoat', the story of a clerk who gains a new lease of life with the acquisition of a new cloak, only to have it stolen – an event which results in his premature death. The volume also includes a short dramatic piece, *Upon Leaving the Theatre After the Performance of a New Comedy*, set among members of an audience who are leaving the theatre after a performance of *The Government Inspector*. In it Gogol uses the characters to express his views on the nature of comedy, especially the function of laughter, and the state of contemporary theatre in general.

His play, *Marriage*, is performed in Moscow with his one-act play, *Gamblers*, as a curtain-raiser. The latter continues the swindling motif of *Dead Souls*. In this case a card-sharper, Ikharev, sets out in concert with a gang of fellow card-players to fool an apparent innocent who turns out to be another member of the gang. As a result Ikharev is ingeniously and unsuspectingly robbed of his money.

From May to December visits Germany and Nice, where he calls on A.O. Smirnova, his 'spiritual sister' and one of many (usually older) women with whom he has platonic relationships and who play influential roles in his life.

Death of his eldest sister, Maria.

1845 Ill in Frankfurt in May; further signs of the psychotic condition which points to his early death. In the summer, he burns the first draft of the second part of *Dead Souls*.

1846 Writes 'The Denouement of *The Government Inspector*', which seeks to explain the play in allegorical terms.

1847 Publishes *Selected Passages from Correspondence with Friends*, consisting of thirty-two essays on matters social, domestic, artistic and literary, characterised by a tone of religiosity and conservatism. It also contains the polemical essay 'On the Theatre, on the One-sided View Towards the Theatre, and on One-sidedness in General', which contains the famous statement that theatre 'is a kind of rostrum from which much good can be spoken to the world'.

Publishes *An Author's Confession* and *Meditations Upon Divine Liturgy*.

Begins his association with Father Matvei Konstaninovski who tries to persuade him of the evils of literature and get Gogol to repent and enter a monastery.

Between June and August exchanges polemical letters with Belinski in response to the latter's denunciation of *Selected Passages* in his famous 'Letter to Gogol'.

1848 Lives at various times in Moscow, Odessa and
–52   Petersburg. Having felt destined from an early age to achieve great things, Gogol's religious obsessions seem to intensify at around this time when he visits

several monasteries. His bouts of psychotic illness also intensify.

1848   Manifesting a complete lack of interest in the revolutionary events of Europe, which he later denounces, Gogol sets out in February on a pilgrimage to the Holy Land and Jerusalem accompanied by his former schoolmate, Konstantin Bazili, now a diplomat based in Syria. The visit does not live up to expectations.

1851   Meets Turgenev, whose plays of the 1840s may be said to show the influence of Gogol.

1852   During the night of 11/12 February burns the second draft of Part Two of *Dead Souls*.

21 February. Gogol dies at 8.00 a.m. having, under Father Matvei's influence, submitted himself to a penitential fast and virtually starved himself to death. This has been preceded by a form of medical torture administered by a council of five doctors, one of whom, Dr Tarasenkov, reports (in a manner which, ironically, recalls the treatment of Poprishchin in 'Diary of a Madman'):

> I left so as not to witness the torturing of the sufferer. When I returned three hours later, at six in the evening, the patient had already been bathed and six large leeches were being placed on his nostrils; . . . And as they applied the leeches he kept on saying, 'Take the leeches off! Take the leeches away!' . . . After seven o'clock, Auver and Klimenkov arrived and ordered the blood-letting to continue a little longer . . . Their treatment of him was pitiless; they handled him like a madman, shouted at him as if he were a living dead thing.

24 February. Gogol's body is buried in the cemetery of the Danilov monastery in Moscow.

Plot

Act One, Scene One

The action of the play is set in a remote Russian provincial town – so remote, in fact, that 'You could gallop for three years without reaching a foreign country.' The curtain rises on a room in the Mayor's house to which a group of town officials has been summoned to listen to the reading of a letter from a relative of the Mayor's which warns of a Government Inspector who is travelling in the area incognito and likely to descend on them at any minute. The officials are horrified and the Mayor sets about advising them on how to prepare for this surprise visitation. In so doing, it becomes apparent that the town and its institutions are in a fairly desperate state. The local court is in disarray, the clerk is drunk, and geese roam at large in the vestibule; the Judge and the Mayor take bribes; in the hospital the standards of hygiene are non-existent and the doctor is an incompetent who doesn't speak the language; the school seems to be full of teachers who are grotesque or eccentric enthusiasts, where they aren't actually demented; the streets are overflowing with rubbish and the police are either drunk, or violent, or both. The postal system is under the control of an official who regularly intercepts private correspondence and reads it out of curiosity – a practice which the Mayor now begs him to continue in the hope of discovering something from the Government Inspector. Two almost identical landowners arrive at this point. They have been lunching at the local inn and claim to have identified the Government Inspector who, it seems, is not a recent arrival but has been living there for almost two weeks and so has had plenty of time to note the true state of affairs in the town before remedial measures have been put in

train. In a state of panic, the Mayor prepares to meet the
Inspector by donning full-dress uniform, while issuing last-
minute orders to the Police Superintendent. He departs for
the inn accompanied by the two landowners, Bobchinsky
and Dobchinsky. His state of genuine anxiety is signalled
by his confusing his words and donning a hatbox instead
of a hat. The scene concludes with the arrival of the
Mayor's wife and daughter, excited at the news of the
arrival of a Government Inspector but more concerned
about his looks than with his power to unmask corruption.

Act One, Scene Two
The scene is set in a poky room under the stairs at the
local inn where an impecunious St Petersburg clerk,
Khlyestakov, and his illiterate but wily manservant, Ossip,
are staying. In an opening soliloquy, Ossip establishes the
facts about his master's real identity, that the latter has no
money (having lost it at cards), is prone to give himself
airs and live above his very low station in life. They are
both hungry and denied food because they are unable to
pay the hotel bill. From Ossip's point of view, St
Petersburg is a highly desirable place to live compared to
this provincial backwater. Khlyestakov arrives, having been
for a walk, which has only served to increase his hunger
pangs. He pleads with Ossip to order some lunch.
Eventually, this appears in the form of soup and some
roasted meat which Khlyestakov devours avidly while never
ceasing to complain about both the food and the service.
The Mayor's arrival is announced and, assuming that he is
about to be carted off to prison for non-payment of his
bill, Khlyestakov is as terrified of the imminent encounter
as the Mayor is of confronting a supposedly irate
government official. From an audience's point of view, the
comedy of the ensuing scene is intensified by a sense of
their mutual misunderstanding. The interview is conducted
in the presence of Dobchinsky and overheard by
Bobchinsky who, throughout, keeps opening the door and

peeping in. Khlyestakov reveals his impecuniousness which
the Mayor takes to be an obvious lie and a discreet way of
eliciting a bribe, offered by the Mayor in the form of 'a
loan' to enable Khlyestakov to pay his hotel bill.

Khlyestakov starts bragging about his father's estate in
Saratov and his own lifestyle in St Petersburg. The Mayor
remains convinced that Khlyestakov is the Government
Inspector but is willing to go along with his wish to remain
incognito. The scene is brought to a head by the Mayor's
offer to take 'the Government Inspector' to view the school
and the hospital, following which the distinguished visitor
is to be a guest at the Mayor's own house, the plan being
to get Khlyestakov so drunk that he reveals his intentions.
The Mayor writes a note to his wife asking her to prepare
for the Government Inspector's arrival but, before they
leave, the door caves in and Bobchinsky comes flying into
the room with it, much to the Mayor's consternation and
the former's chagrin. Khlyestakov is singularly unfazed by
the incident and merely enquires as to the extent of
Bobchinsky's injuries.

Act One, Scene Three
The action returns to the room in the Mayor's house
where his wife and daughter are still standing at the
window where they were left at the end of Scene One.
Dobchinsky arrives with the Mayor's note and gives an
account of the interview he has just witnessed, to the
obvious excitement of the two women who begin to argue
with each other over which dresses to wear that evening. A
short scene follows between the Mayor's houseboy,
Mishka, and Ossip who is delivering his master's things
from the inn and who confirms his master's importance,
while contriving to wangle a decent meal for himself.
Khlyestakov and the town officials arrive at the Mayor's
house fresh from wining and dining with Khlyestakov who
is feeling the effects of it. The Mayor talks hypocritically
about the rigours of his official position and his elevated

sense of responsibility, before introducing his wife and
daughter to Khlyestakov who, as if on cue, instantly adopts
the manner of a lounge lizard-cum-gigolo, much to the
excitement of the women, whom he compliments and who
press him for information on his tastes and talents. These
emerge to be commensurate with those of well-known
novelists and poets, including Pushkin, with whom
Khlyestakov claims to be on intimate terms. Khlyestakov
then embarks on the longest speech in the play in which
his powers of inspirational exaggeration, fuelled by alcohol
intake, lay claim to positions of power and influence in the
land second only to the Tsar himself. He is not so much
telling lies as responding to the cringing respect being
accorded his person. His increasingly wild peroration,
which reveals the downtrodden clerk beneath the
exaggerated claims to elevated status, terrifies the officials
and confuses the Mayor even further. If the alcohol was
designed to get the Inspector to reveal himself, it has had
the effect of revealing more than the Mayor can cope with.
The scene concludes with Khlyestakov's inebriated
collapse, before being ushered solicitously into an adjoining
bedroom, uttering the name of the rare fish he has been
fed for lunch, 'Salted cod!' The response of the women to
this megalomaniacal display has been quite different to that
of the men, in that they regard the performance as a form
of sexual display aimed at them. The way is thus prepared
for Khlyestakov's wooing of both women later. The Mayor
realises that one way of appeasing a Government Inspector
indirectly is to appeal to his servant. Ossip cleverly avoids
giving the game away and willingly accepts money for
anticipated favours.

Act Two
The scene is the same room the following morning, to
which the town officials have summoned themselves, rather
than been summoned, to present formal submissions to the
Government Inspector and to answer for their

responsibilities. Each has come terrified and armed with a bribe but uncertain as to how it will be received if offered. Sounds of movement in the adjoining room lead to the panicky exit of the officials before Khlyestakov emerges, still suffering the effects of whatever he drank the day before which, as the Mayor says, would have toppled an elephant. Manifesting remarkable powers of recovery, Khlyestakov proceeds to interview the officials in turn. Each departs in relief, having given him considerable sums of money which they interpret as bribes but which he regards, first as unsolicited, then as solicited loans. We gain further insight into the nature of the officials as each is interviewed by Khlyestakov, ranging from the extreme nervousness of the schoolmaster to the insidious Charity Commissioner who is only too willing to inform on his colleagues and, typically, loath to part with any money. The 'bribe scenes' conclude with an interview between Khlyestakov and the two landowners, one of whom pathetically wishes an illegitimate child to be made legitimate, while the other, even more pathetically, just wishes to be mentioned in court circles as 'existing'. They are the only ones who are not armed with a bribe and, when asked for a loan, can only muster sixty-five roubles between them.

The true nature of his situation has begun to dawn on Khlyestakov, who decides to write a letter to his friend in St Petersburg describing what has happened to him and regaling his friend, who has literary ambitions, with the story. Ossip, who has already realised the misunderstanding of his master's position, suggests they depart before they are found out, but they are interrupted by a group of local shopkeepers, led by one Abdullin, who seek redress of grievances against the Mayor for requisitioning from them at will whichever commodities he fancies, without payment. Blandly promising to attend to their complaints, Khlyestakov is next confronted by the locksmith's wife and the sergeant's widow who also have grounds for complaint against the Mayor, the former being exceptionally and

comically vociferous in voicing hers. Again, Khlyestakov
casually agrees to do something about it and, with their
departure, a host of hands bearing petitions appears
through a window before a door opens to reveal a vista of
downtrodden and impoverished peasantry. In mild
desperation, Khlyestakov calls for horses to be brought but
is suddenly faced with the Mayor's daughter, who has
entered the room, and whom he promptly tries to seduce,
much to her apparent discomfiture. His efforts are
interrupted by the Mayor's wife, who manifests outrage at
her daughter's behaviour, expels her from the room and
then proceeds to succumb to Khlyestakov's redirected
blandishments. In a mirror-like sequence, Khlyestakov's
wooing of the mother is interrupted by the daughter,
whose hand Khlyestakov then begs in marriage, winking at
the mother to indicate that this is a strategy. The Mayor is
informed of the marriage proposal, but hardly has time to
take in this extraordinary piece of good news before Ossip
arrives to announce that the horses are ready and it is time
to depart. Khlyestakov explains that it is only for a day or
so, to receive his uncle's blessing on the union, and seizes
the opportunity to borrow still more money from his future
father-in-law. The scene concludes with his off-stage
departure to the sound of carriage bells, never to be seen
again.

   The Mayor and his wife now contemplate the good life
once their daughter is married to an important court
official and they have taken up residence in the capital.
Having learned of the shopkeepers' attempt to tarnish his
reputation by denouncing him to Khlyestakov, the Mayor
has summoned them for a bout of bullying, now that his
good fortune has had the effect of turning the tables on
them. They depart suitably browbeaten, with their tails
between their legs. Meanwhile, news of the engagement of
the Mayor's daughter has spread rapidly and the town
officials, accompanied in some cases by their wives, arrive
to present their congratulations, along with a few
dignitaries who are making their first appearance in the

play. It becomes clear that not all are happy with the
family's good news, while wife and daughter compete as to
whom the fiancé threatened suicide over if his marriage
proposal was rejected. The Mayor has a sneezing fit and
accepts the offered blessings before the Postmaster hurries
in with the news that he has dared to steam open a letter
from the Government Inspector only to discover the awful
truth that the latter is nothing of the sort. Unable to
believe it at first, and threatening either to arrest the
Postmaster or have him sent to Siberia, the Mayor is
finally forced to listen to a reading of the letter in which
he and his fellow officials are shamelessly lampooned by
Khlyestakov, who says he is going to follow his friend's
example and become a writer. The Mayor furiously berates
himself, an experienced swindler, at being out-swindled.
He imagines his situation becoming the subject of a play
and suddenly addresses the audience with unexpected
ferocity, 'What are you laughing at? You're laughing at
yourselves!' He then demands to know who it was first
circulated the news that the nonentity at the inn was a
Government Inspector. He and the others round on
Bobchinsky and Dobchinsky, who first deny responsibility
and then begin to accuse each other. At this moment, a
gendarme enters and announces the arrival of a real
Government Inspector who awaits them at the inn. This
produces 'a tableau of consternation' before the curtain
falls.

Commentary

Theatrical context

The achievement represented by *The Government Inspector* is even more remarkable when placed in the context of theatrical development in Russia in the early nineteenth century. There was no professional Russian theatre of any significance until the late eighteenth century, unlike other European countries which had experienced the cultural impact of the Renaissance in the sixteenth century. Russia remained a medieval country far removed both from the Renaissance and, indeed, from most of the Enlightenment movement of the eighteenth century. It was only during the reign of Peter the Great (1682–1725) that a form of professional theatre was first introduced into Russia, his example being followed, later in the century, by Catherine the Great (1762–96).

The first theatre companies to perform in Russia were imported from abroad and plays tended to be acted either in French or in German. The repertoire was also foreign, and plays by Russian writers, largely imitative of European neo-classical models, did not begin to get written or performed until the latter half of the eighteenth century. There were also no indigenous theatre companies until Catherine the Great decided to create them and no acting schools. However, the practice which emerged and persisted for the next hundred years, until 1882, was one dominated by the Russian court which exercised almost total control over both theatres and dramatic repertoire. The situation was not unlike that which existed in England between 1737 and 1843, when court control was exercised over the only theatres which were permitted to perform plays. In England's case this right was extended to the so-called Patent Houses, Covent Garden and Drury Lane. As

far as Russia was concerned, the royal prerogative extended
only to the Imperial Aleksandrinsky Theatre in St
Petersburg and the Maly Theatre in Moscow. The other
two Imperial theatres, the Mariinsky in St Petersburg and
the Bolshoi in Moscow were better known for ballet and
opera performances.

The plays which native Russian dramatists began to
write, and which were staged at the end of the eighteenth
and the beginning of the nineteenth centuries, are
unremarkable and have largely been forgotten. They
consisted mainly of tragedies which were pale imitations of
neo-classical French examples as represented by the work
of Racine and Corneille and were influenced by French
neo-classical theory. The Russian language was not
considered fit to express elevated thoughts and feelings
because it was essentially an oral language spoken by the
peasantry. The written language was Church Slavonic and
confined to religious literature, with the result that the only
linguistic model for tragic expression was either French or
German, or a Russian which was both unnatural and
stilted. This situation did not change until Pushkin, with
his tragedy *Boris Godunov*, abandoned the European neo-
classical heritage in favour of the less inhibiting example of
Shakespeare.

It was comedy which proved to be the path which
Russian dramatists pursued with most success and which
has proved to be the case to this day. The tradition was
initiated by Denis Fonvizin, whose plays *The Brigadier*
(dating from the 1760s) and *The Minor* (first performed in
1782) showed that it was possible to write successful
dramas in the Russian language which were rooted in a
very specific Russian reality. Fonvizin's example was taken
up by others although, prior to Gogol, the greatest impact
was made by Aleksandr Griboyedov's verse comedy *Gore ot
uma*, usually translated as *Woe from Wit*, first performed in
1830.

The major influence on Russian comedy was Molière
who, in turn, was indebted to Italian comedy, the

commedia dell'arte, with its stock types, including the braggart and the clever servant, to whom the characters of Khlyestakov and Ossip may be said to correspond to some degree. However, by the 1830s, a more genteel style of comedy dominated the Russian stage, imported from the West, whose imitators included M. Zagoskin, one of whose works Khlyestakov lays claim to in Gogol's play. Gogol was also familiar with a Ukrainian tradition of popular religious drama, as well as fairground farce and the puppet show, and had read a good deal of European comic drama, all of which influenced his own work.

The plot of *The Government Inspector* is said to have been given to Gogol by Pushkin and was based on something which happened to the poet, on his travels researching material for a book on the Pugachev Rebellion. However, it was also a familiar tale of mistaken identity which, in dramatic terms, went back as far as the Latin drama of Plautus, as well as that of Shakespeare, Molière and others. Nearer home, the fabulist Ivan Krylov (who was present at the first performance of *The Government Inspector*) had himself written a play *A Lesson for Daughters* (1806/7) in which someone passes himself off as a marquis. The plot is also based on the receipt of a letter which gives rise to expectations which lead to the identification of the wrong person as someone of high estate. Similarly, in a play by Nikolai Khmelnitsky, *Castles in the Air* (1818), a person who is not a count is taken for one until a servant discovers the truth. In A.N. Verstovsky's vaudeville *The Madhouse*, the plot may be said to resemble that of Gogol's play where a doctor's daughter's fiancé is mistaken for an asylum patient. The situation is resolved by a servant who, at the end, announces the arrival of the real madman. There was even an earlier play entitled *Government Inspectors, or The Grass is Always Greener on the Other Side* (1832) in which a provincial town awaits the arrival of government officials with fear and trembling only to succeed in bribing them and emerging unscathed from the experience. A play by G.F. Kvitka, *A Visitor from the*

Capital, written in 1827 but not published until 1840, has many plot similarities with Gogol's play (Gippius, 1989, pp.83-4).

The traditions which came to characterise Russian dramatic performance, with their emphasis on the craft of the actor and the importance of the director and designer, did not really come to fruition until the late nineteenth century and the emergence of Stanislavsky. He himself had been influenced by the earlier writings on the subject by the dramatist Aleksandr Ostrovsky who, in his turn, looked back to Turgenev and Gogol. However, the situation in Gogol's day was far from ideal, with very little attention being paid to the importance of rehearsal, *mise-en-scène* or the notion that drama and performance were serious art forms to be set alongside those of music and dance. The situation in the theatre during Gogol's lifetime was described by the radical critic, Belinsky, who championed Gogol the dramatist and was especially appreciative of *The Government Inspector*:

> Plays which delight the bulk of the Aleksandrinsky audiences are divided into the poetic and the comic. The former are either translations of monstrous German dramas composed of sentimentalities, trivial effects and false situations, or homespun compositions in which inflated phraseology and soulless exclamations degrade time-honoured historical names. Songs, dances, opportunely or inopportunely providing a favourite actress with a pretext for singing and dancing, as well as insanity scenes, are inevitable components of this kind of drama, which evokes clamours of delight and rages of applause. Comic pieces are invariably either translations of, or adaptations from French vaudevilles. These plays altogether stamped out both stagecraft and dramatic taste in the Russian theatre. (B.V. Varneke, *History of the Russian Theatre*, 2nd ed., New York, Hafner Publishing Co., 1971, p.295)

It was in this climate that Gogol set about formulating a theory of drama and, again at the suggestion of Pushkin, began a study of the history of dramatic theory and criticism. He proposed a programme whereby the Russian spectator would be able to become familiar with the best products of European drama. He attacked the tendencies which had led to the dominance in the theatre of superficial forms, inveighing against the genres of vaudeville (a type of drama imported from France and using simple verse forms as well as song and dance) and melodrama. Gogol wanted a Russian theatre with an independent repertoire which presented plays concerned with national life:

> The position of Russian actors is pitiful . . . What are they to do with these strange heroes, who are neither French nor German, but some sort of unbalanced people having absolutely no definite passion or clear-cut physiognomy? . . . For God's sake, give us Russian characters, give us *our own selves*, our swindlers, our cranks! Onto the stage with them, for the people to laugh at! (N.V. Gogol, 'Petersburg Notes of 1836', *Russian Literature Tri-Quarterly*, VII, 1974, p.183)

For Gogol, the theatre represented the means for the education of an entire nation. It was 'a rostrum from which a lively lesson is read to an entire crowd at once, where . . . a familiar but concealed vice is revealed and to the secret voice of general participation a familiar, timidly hiding, lofty emotion is exhibited' (ibid., p.184).

He wrote about the significant function of laughter in *After the Play* or, to give it its full title, *Upon Leaving the Theatre after the Performance of a New Comedy*, where he characterised three different modes:

1 A light laughter which serves for the idle amusement and entertainment of people.
2 A laughter which is aroused by temporary irritation and a morbid, jaundiced disposition.
3 Laughter which issues wholly from man's bright nature, issues from it because at bottom there is an inexhaustible well which deepens everything, draws attention to what might have passed unnoticed and without whose penetrating force man would have been disheartened by life's trivialities and life's emptiness.

(N.V. Gogol, *After the Play*, *Tulane Drama Review*, Winter 1959)

Tracing the history of comic writing he asserted that, at first, comedy was a social and popular form as shown in the work of Aristophanes. Later, comedy entered the narrow path of portraying the private and individual, of which the love intrigue was an essential part (you will note the absence of this element in *The Government Inspector*). He puts his own point of view in the words of the Second Lover of the Arts in *After the Play*:

> The most important theme in the plot of a play is the desire to obtain a good position, to outshine and eclipse your rival by the brilliance of your wit, to avenge yourself for being disregarded or laughed at. Does not rank, money or a good marriage mean more to us today than love?

The final sentence has been seen as programmatic of Gogol's drama as a whole, focusing on three main themes of his major plays: rank (*The Government Inspector*), marriage (the play with that title), and money (*Gamblers*). In Gogol's concept of the social function of the theatre, there is an anticipation of the theories of the Russian Symbolists, expressed at the turn of the twentieth century, to the effect that the theatre can exercise a semi-religious function similar to that which existed in fifth-century Athens, in serving to reinforce a sense of social and spiritual unity. As Gogol expressed it:

> The theatre is by no means a trifle, nor a petty thing, if you take into consideration that it can accommodate a crowd of five or six thousand persons all at once, and that this multitude whose members taken singly have nothing in common, can suddenly be shaken by the same shock, sob with the same tears, and laugh with the same general laughter. It is a kind of rostrum from which much good can be spoken to the world. (N.V. Gogol, 'On the Theatre, On the One-Sided View Towards the Theatre, and on One-Sidedness in General', in Gogol, 1969, p.75)

Structure and style

The Government Inspector is a masterpiece of artistic unity.
The Mayor's terse opening announcement plunges the
audience instantly into the action, arousing interest and
curiosity as the impact of the news on the assembled
officials, their instant fear and panic, sets the tone for the
whole piece. In Nabokov's words:

> The play begins with a blinding flash of lightning and ends in a
> thunderclap. In fact it is wholly placed in the tense gap between
> the flash and the crash. (Nabokov, 1961, p.42)

Gogol varies the pace of the action throughout the play.
After the Mayor's initial bombshell, the first act unfolds
relatively slowly as the true state of affairs in the town is
revealed, through the instructions the Mayor gives in order
to pull the wool over the eyes of the visiting official by
creating a façade of good order. After Bobchinsky and
Dobchinsky report seeing Khlyestakov at the inn the pace
speeds up as the Mayor is galvanised into action. In
varying the pace between, and within, scenes Gogol
develops several unexpected twists and turns, each of
which propels the action forward. He maintains tension
and generates mounting excitement for the audience as the
plot moves inexorably via a series of comic situations
towards its climax and resolution when the townspeople
realise their misconception. The play is remarkably
compact.

The comedy is founded on mutual fear and
misunderstanding and Gogol reflects this in the way in
which he structures the exposition of the play by dividing
the transfer of necessary background information to the
audience via the two sets of protagonists. In the first
exposition (Act One, Scene One, pp.11–17), the Mayor
and his associates reveal their own malpractice, whereas in
the second (Act One, Scene Two, pp.26–33), the truth
about Khlyestakov and his situation is presented, largely
through the wry observations of his servant, Ossip. Both
expositions end at a point of tension – in the first the

Mayor learns that Khlyestakov is staying at the inn and, in the second, Khlyestakov is told that the Mayor has arrived to pay a 'courtesy call'. In each case one character misunderstands the reason for the other's presence.

The nub of the plot is the case of mistaken identity which creates a situation of dramatic irony, with only the audience knowing the full extent of the misunderstandings, and which runs almost to the very end of the play. The initial error opens up comic possibilities which Gogol exploits to the full. The greatest intensity of comic verbal invention occurs in the central sections of the play, for example when the Mayor and the Charity Commissioner try to outdo each other in praising their own corrupt practices (pp.46–7) and when Khlyestakov holds the stage while building a progressively more detailed and outrageous description of his supposed life in St Petersburg (pp.49–52).

The shape of the whole play is symmetrical. Its opening and conclusion are both brief and dramatic; it closes as it begins with a group scene in which the arrival of a government official is announced. The action opens with the reading of one letter just as the dénouement is precipitated by the reading of another. At the end of the comedy the townspeople are transfixed with horror at the thought that the catastrophe they had thought they were avoiding throughout the play, now seems about to happen. The gendarme's arrival, giving a final twist to the plot, is a true *coup de théâtre* but does not really fulfil Gogol's stated aim of showing the law triumphant, because the punishment that might be expected of the corruption displayed by the officials is not seen to be carried out. Although the final tableau, which Gogol wished to last for one and a half minutes (see note to p.97), is extremely difficult to achieve, and in practice the curtain falls after less than 20 seconds, the Gendarme's appearance ensures that everything remains uncertain and menacing. Critics continue to argue over whether Gogol leads his audience to draw the expected political conclusions that corruption in public life will be uncovered and punished or whether the play's moral is more open than Gogol's avowed intention of showing the law punishing evildoers.

Gogol's belief, which went against the theatrical conventions of his time, that in writing a satirical social comedy he would enlighten as well as entertain his audience, did not mean that he automatically rejected all established dramatic techniques, more that he reshaped them to suit his own purposes. In fact, in many respects the play is conventional in structure. Although Gogol rejected the hackneyed plot of cardboard lovers and the inevitable happy ending, he largely observed the three classical unities of time, place and action and uses asides and soliloquies in traditional ways.

Gogol makes sparing use of physical comedy, largely avoiding the purely physical jokes that characterise farce. He does use physical comedy in the wooing scenes in order to parody popular sentimental drama but the physical aspects of the humour are largely used to extend individual characterisation at particular points. For example, when the Mayor is about to don a hatbox instead of his hat, this reveals the depth of his agitation. Bobchinsky's and Dobchinsky's antics, including the collapsing door at the inn, are used to illustrate their desire to please and flatter, not simply to raise a laugh.

The real humour of the play arises from its dialogue, which develops the potential of the misunderstandings of the plot, while creating individual ways of speaking for each character to underline and reveal contrasting values and attitudes. Gogol's achievement in breaking down the barriers between written and spoken Russian is highly praised by all critics, who acknowledge his influence in forging a theatrical language which sounds like everyday speech and yet uses aspects of literary style to make idiosyncratic expression to suit each character. Every time Gogol revised the text he edited words and phrases to refine this process, thus creating 'a gallery of memorable, sharply drawn characters, each with his or her own voice' (Beresford, 1997, p.68).

The Mayor, for example, is the most important of the officials and shows the greatest ability to adapt the way he speaks to suit each situation. He rants and bullies the other officials, exerting his authority with ironic politeness, or flatters and fawns when with Khlyestakov, using appropriately official expressions. With members of his family he can be coarse and abusive. This deliberate controlling of his way of speaking enables the audience to appreciate the character's hypocrisy and self-seeking nature – he will always adapt to get the most out of any situation he is in. By contrast the other officials each have one characteristic mode of expression: the Judge, who thinks he's well-read but is in fact deplorably ignorant, uses short, simple sentences for maximum effect; the Charity Commissioner, who is devious and sycophantic, wheedles and ingratiates himself in unctuous, alternately honeyed and coarse, tones; the Schools Superintendent, a timid creature terrified of causing offence, hardly dares to open his mouth.

In complete contrast to these local officials is Khlyestakov whose mercurial speech mirrors his fluid character. His expression changes as his mind flits from one subject to another. Like the Mayor, he can vary his tone according to his audience. His speech contains many elements, ranging from colloquial to civil service jargon to card players' slang. At times he seems almost drunk on the language he is using, particularly when bragging to the officials, who are intimidated by his megalomaniacal flights of fancy and stunned into silence. He can transform himself through words into a commanding and magnificent figure because he believes his own words. The audience can see the impact of what he says on himself and his listeners, while at the same time retaining their own understanding of his true character.

Gogol's use of hyperbole is a key linguistic feature and a typical device of the play. It is used most effectively by Ossip, who says he's so hungry 'my belly must think my throat's been cut!' ('my stomach's rumbling like a regimental band', in the original); and by the Mayor who defines the remoteness of his provincial town by claiming that it is three years' gallop from any frontier; but most of all, by Khlyestakov, particularly in the bragging scene when he speaks about the lavish entertainment on offer at the balls in St Petersburg, citing the example of a huge water-melon costing 700 roubles. That such exaggerations are accepted without question by his listeners underscores their gullible servility as well as Khlyestakov's over-fertile but essentially earthbound imagination.

Repetition is the most frequently used linguistic device. In the opening scenes for example, the words 'inspector' and 'incognito' resound, underlining the impact of the news on the officials, and Gogol exploits to humorous effect Bobchinsky's repetition of Dobchinsky's interruptions to his rambling account (pp.18–20). In the bribery scenes each official uses, in the original text, the same formal words on entering – 'I have the honour to introduce myself' – and on leaving – 'I will not presume to intrude on you further' – as well as using stock phrases that indicate no individuality of response. In this way Gogol uses the technique of repetition to diminish the humanity of these corrupt officials, reducing them to mechanical automata. Similarly Gogol uses comparisons with the animal world to undermine the status of the characters. Thus the current translators have Khlyestakov describe his own father as being 'as stupid as a mule' (p.37) and refer to Anna Andreyevna as 'the old hen herself' (p.60), who in turn accuses her own daughter of 'dashing in like a scalded cat' (p.78). The Mayor berates the shopkeepers as 'two-faced misbegotten store-rats' (p.84) and terms Khlyestakov a 'jumped-up little worm' (p.95).

Gogol followed the well-established comic tradition of creating tag names for characters to exemplify their key characteristic, in this case often providing ironic counterparts to the qualities that would normally be associated with the function of the character. For example, the Schools Superintendent's name, Khlopov, is derived from the verb 'to slap' and Lyapkin-Tyapkin's name comes from a phrase used to describe something done rapidly and any-old-how.

In writing his play in this way Gogol was setting a precedent in Russian drama. As we've said, until this time plays had been written in artificial literary language that had little to do with the life led by ordinary people. These innovations partly explain the high position Gogol holds in the opinions of scholars and critics. Unfortunately his use of language is so subtle and varied that it poses great problems for translators, who struggle to find genuine equivalents for Gogol's imaginative variety and combination of idioms and expressions.

Characters

Gogol condemned the type of characterisation that featured in contemporary melodrama and farce. However, opinion is sharply divided over the question of whether Gogol's method of creating character produced distorted grotesques or recognisably real people. In 1842 Nikolai Polevoi referred to Gogol's 'ugly grotesques', whereas a year later Belinsky described them as 'people, not puppets' with characteristics that were 'drawn from the innermost recesses of Russian life'. This debate has continued ever since, not surprisingly since there is obviously truth in both opinions. Gogol does not seek to create fully rounded characters as might be found in a Tolstoy novel but neither are his characters simply 'puppets whose precariously contrived mode of existence is pointed up by their blatantly comic names' (V. Erlich, *Gogol*, New Haven and London, Yale, 1969, p.103).

In 1846 Gogol wrote 'A Warning to those who would

play "The Government Inspector" properly', in which his advice to actors underlines the acting style he desired for his play:

> The main thing to guard against is caricature. There should be nothing exaggerated or trite, even in the minor roles. On the contrary, the actor should try particularly to be more modest, more simple and noble, so to speak, than the person he is playing really is. The less the actor tries to play for laughs, the more he will reveal the comic nature of the part he is playing. The humour will emerge spontaneously from the very seriousness with which each of the persons portrayed in the comedy is occupied with his own concerns. They are all busily, even feverishly, pursuing their own affairs as if these were the most important things in their lives. Only the spectator, from his detached position, can see how futile their concerns are.

In seeking to meet this objective, Gogol accentuated particular features and magnified their verbal idiosyncrasies. Consequently, the characters of *The Government Inspector* possess exaggerated but nevertheless very human traits. They are not grotesque monsters but unmistakable human types who are to be found in societies everywhere in conditions that may be quite different from the Russia of his time. Gogol explained his approach to his characters clearly when writing about Khlyestakov:

> In short, this man should be a type embodying many things found separately in different Russian characters, but here combined fortuitously in one person, as very often happens in real life. Each of us becomes or has become a Khlyestakov at least for a moment, if not several moments, only naturally we do not care to admit it. We even like to make fun of the fact, but of course only when we see Khlyestakov in someone else, not ourselves. (Extract from a letter)

Gogol provided Notes on several of the main characters for the 1842 edition of the play. These are reproduced on pp.5–7 of the current edition and should be read in conjunction with the following interpretations.

Khlyestakov, a government clerk

According to Nabokov (1961, p.55) Khlyestakov's very name 'is a stroke of genius, for it conveys to the Russian reader an effect of lightness and rashness, a prattling tongue, the swish of a slim walking cane, the slapping sound of playing cards, the braggadocio of a nincompoop and the dashing ways of a ladykiller'.

Khlyestakov is a junior civil servant from a landowning family of modest means, who desperately wants to be a fashionable trendsetter at the heart of St Petersburg society. He is a poseur who cannot help but show off, always attempting to impress others. Although he is an opportunist who takes advantage of the situation of mistaken identity in which he finds himself, he is essentially passive, reacting to events around him. He lives entirely in the present without a thought for the possible consequences of any of his actions. His speech reflects his character – he gabbles, uses disjointed and often incomplete sentences as his mind jumps from one subject to another. His tone and manner of speaking vary depending upon his mood and the person he is addressing. Sometimes he is polite and deferential, at others over-familiar and impudent. He grovels to, blusters at, and hectors others in rapid succession. He shows just how silly he is when seeking to impress the Mayor's wife and daughter when he tries to use French phrases and exaggerated politeness, but he can stun his listeners into awed silence when he launches into hyperbolic descriptions of his imagined place in fashionable society. At all times he revels in being the centre of attention.

It is important to note that Gogol did not seek to create Khlyestakov as a stage villain. His lies are not conscious deceptions but simply the fantastic, self-deceiving outpourings of his ego; Khlyestakov, wanting to be able to 'pluck the flowers of pleasure', fails to perceive the normal boundaries between the real and the imaginary, as if he is intoxicated by the effects of his own words, carried away by his own imagination. Gogol carefully developed Khlyestakov's character so that he is not just a theatrical cheat and braggart. Unlike the normal stage villain he remains unaware for a considerable time of the potential profit he could accumulate from being mistaken for a government inspector. Khlyestakov is essentially an empty shell, a nothingness into and from which fantasies can stream to fill the vacuum that is at his core:

> it is the unearned, misdirected adulation which emerges from these craven fools, along with his own mounting intoxication, that sucks the babbling guest of honour into an orgy of daydreaming, and flamboyant enactment of ludicrous fantasies of omnipotence. Khlyestakov is a nobody, literally a nobody, propelled into the limelight by the inanity and panic . . . by the bad faith of the local bureaucrats. (V. Erlich, *Gogol*, 1969, p.105)

Ossip, his servant

The name Ossip is a colloquial form of Iosif (Joseph), hence 'Joe'. He is a canny peasant who has lived long enough in St Petersburg to acquire a semblance of urban sophistication in the way he speaks. In the original text Gogol makes him mispronounce words like 'theatre' and 'avenue' and gives him some self-consciously learned vocabulary. His monologue at the beginning of Act One, Scene Two, establishes his perspective of life with Khlyestakov, his naturally ironic cheekiness and slangy way of speaking, as well as ensuring that the audience acquire the factual knowledge they need as part of the vital exposition. In this sense Ossip is a convenient tool for the playwright. He is one in a long tradition of cheeky, knowing servants whose observations on their apparent betters provide an opportunity for chorus-like commentary by the dramatist.

The Mayor, Skvoznik Dmukhanovsky

The post of Mayor or Governor of a provincial town, with wide powers over the police, the military and public works, was created by Catherine the Great. A Mayor had two types of uniform for different occasions, the first worn on duty (undress: frock-coat and top hat), the second on special occasions (full dress). In Act Two the Mayor is in full dress with a black cocked hat with silver tassels at each end and with a sword belt and sword.

The Mayor's name has meaningful associations and could be hyphenated to suggest the character's pomposity. A *skvoznik* is a 'draught' (as of wind) and also figuratively means 'a sly old fox' or 'an experienced swindler'. *Dmukhnuti* means 'to blow' (again as of wind) in Ukrainian so the name combines 'windbag' with 'swindler'.

Primarily interested in personal gain and because he has always had an eye to the main chance, the Mayor has never taken a hard look at himself. He seems unaware of his oppressive bullying attitude since his behaviour is not determined by a malicious desire to tyrannise over others but simply to achieve more material advantage for himself. He prays, goes to church and believes himself to be a devout Christian. He is highly conscious of his own manipulative deceitfulness – as he declares boastfully when confronted with his own gullibility (p.95) – but cannot break the habit of acquiring as much as possible. Caught in the trap of his own ambition, the Mayor demonstrates his instinctive wiliness in his ability to adjust his tone and manner of speaking most adroitly, switching from issuing orders to his fellow officials to being extremely deferential when speaking to the supposed Inspector.

The Judge, Lyapkin-Tyapkin

Created to typify the ignorance of Russian magistrates of the time, the Judge is the second most important official of the town. The Judge of the district court dealt with minor crimes committed by members of the gentry. His was an elected post.

He is essentially a pompous ass who is obviously not an appropriate person to sit in judgement on others. He delights in pulling rank on other officials, as shown when he lines them all up in the correct order for their interviews with Khlyestakov and constantly reminds them of the punishments that could befall them if the authorities catch them out. His real passion is for hare coursing, and he is apparently oblivious to the chaos that is his courtroom. Appropriately, his name is derived from the phrase *lyap-tyap*, used to describe something done rapidly and any-old-how.

The Charity Commissioner, Zemlyanika

Vladimir Nabokov describes the Charity Commissioner, whose name literally means 'wild strawberry', as 'Mr Strawberry – an overripe brown strawberry wounded by the lip of a frog' (1961, p.43). The post was that of director of charitable institutions such as almshouses, orphanages and hospitals, which were not in fact run by charitable organisations but administered by government departments.

Zemlyanika is the most devious and sycophantic of the officials. He wheedles and ingratiates himself while, at the same time, denouncing colleagues behind their backs. He suggests the bribing of Khlyestakov and then makes sure that he goes in last so that he can tell tales about the others without the risk of either being contradicted or informed on himself. His speech varies in tone and vocabulary from smooth and honeyed to extremely coarse, reflecting the duplicity of his character.

The Postmaster, Shpyokin

Very different from the other officials whose main preoccupation is their material advancement, the Postmaster is quite simply nosiness personified. He has an

insatiable curiosity to find out other people's business and
so he opens all of the letters which pass through his hands
– his name is derived from *shpyok*, a term for a police spy.
He has difficulty in expressing his thoughts and feelings, is
easily tongue-tied, speaking in short phrases rather than
coherent sentences. His job would include the provision of
horses and carriages for travellers as well as the collection
and delivery of the post.

The Schools Superintendent, Khlopov

One of the minor officials whom Gogol deemed unworthy
of special comment because 'their originals are . . . always
with us', ironically the person charged with supervising
education in the area is the least articulate, the least able
to express an opinion. He is easily worried by the slightest
thing and absolutely terrified (one assumes with good
cause) lest his schools are inspected.

The derivations of his name are interesting. *Kholop* is a
bond slave or serf and *khlopat* means 'to slap' or 'smack'.
His first name and patronymic are also reminiscent of *luk*
which means 'onion', the vegetable which he is described
as smelling of in Khlyestakov's letter to Tryapichkin.

The District Physician, Hubner

In the original the doctor's name is 'Gibner', a
Russification of the German 'Hübner' but also a reference
to the verg *'gibnut'*, to perish or die. Described by the
Charity Commissioner as a German who 'doesn't
understand a word anyone says' (p.13), Hubner speaks
with a strong accent in largely monosyllabic exclamations
of agreement. His approach to medical care is to leave
things to nature, not bothering to spend money on
expensive medicines. The townspeople's health could
hardly be in the hands of a less suitable person. Beresford
comments: 'By making the doctor a dumb German, Gogol

was appealing to anti-German sentiment. In his time most doctors in Russia, like many other professional men, were Germans who often remained aloof and unrussified, thereby evoking much resentment in the native population' (Gogol, 1996, p.195).

Two landowners, Bobchinsky and Dobchinsky

This comic pair, whom Beresford characterises as 'fussy little pot-bellied squirelings' (1997, p.69), are an example of a common literary device deriving from the *commedia dell'arte*: the comic couple used by writers in many genres – think of Rosencrantz and Guildenstern on the one hand, Tweedledee and Tweedledum on the other. Bobchinsky and Dobchinsky are used by Gogol as instruments to spread the gossip which initiates the misconception of Khlyestakov's identity. Their busybodying sets the whole plot rolling.

Bobchinsky is a bachelor whereas Dobchinsky is a family man, but they have an equal passion for spreading tales around town. Their 'shared' dialogue as they break their news about the stranger at the inn typifies their characters, at the same time as generating humour. They constitute another aspect of the play's themes of doubleness and duality.

Nabokov (1961, p.38) extends Gogol's description of them as having 'little potbellies', to 'they must simply have protruding tummies – pointed little ones like pregnant women have'. Gogol also suggests that Bobchinsky should have dark hair and a light coat in contrast to Dobchinsky's fair hair and dark coat.

The speeches of Dobchinsky and Bobchinsky are interlarded with words which conclude with a hissing sound 's', which is a servile contraction of '*sudar*' (sir). Nabokov explains this as follows: 'The French "sauf votre respect", though much too long, would perhaps render the meaning of the humble little hiss – an abbreviation of

"Soodar" – "Sir" . . . add[ed] to this or that word at the
fall of sentences' (Nabokov, 1961, p.51). Thus Gogol
aurally reinforces the essential servility of this pair of
gossipmongers.

The Mayor's wife, Anna Andreyevna

In a play dominated by male characters, the women,
equally caught up in the corruptness of their social world,
present no alternative sanity. This vain, snobbish mother
fancies herself as irresistible to men, yearns for high-society
life and reveals her pretensions to gentility in her affected
use of words and expressions derived from French, when
in the company of Khlyestakov whom she sees as a way
into the fashionable world. However when she is chastising
her husband or daughter she lapses into a very different,
coarser way of speaking, revealing her essential vulgarity.
Concerned to present herself as being as youthful as
possible, she deliberately creates confusion about her exact
age.

The Mayor's daughter, Maria Antonovna

Dominated by her mother and yet in competition with her,
Maria is very obviously her parents' daughter. She is
flirtatious like her mother but she is also more
straightforward and modest than her mother. She lacks her
mother's self-assurance and appears foolishly naive in her
interpretation of Khlyestakov's attraction to her. She often
blurts out the obvious, for example when stating the name
of the author of the novel Khlyestakov claims to have
written (p.50), failing to understand the elaborate game of
impressing the other party being played by her mother and
their mutual suitor. The contrasts and similarities between
mother and daughter humorously expose to the audience
the pernicious impact of corruption and hypocrisy on the
young.

Intentions and preoccupations

Retrospectively, Gogol explained his intentions in writing *The Government Inspector* in 'An Author's Confession' in 1847:

> I decided to gather in one pile all the bad in Russia of which I was then aware, all the injustices which are committed in those places, and on those occasions where justice above all is demanded of man, and at the same time, to laugh at everything (*Russian Literature Tri-Quarterly*, X, 1974, p.106)

However in 1846 he had made a rather different statement of his intentions in the short didactic conversation piece 'The Denouement of *The Government Inspector*', where he describes the town as symbolising man's soul, the corrupt officials his base passions, and the figure of Khlyestakov as man's awakening conscience. The contrast between these two statements is reflected in the wealth of interpretations of the play to be found in critical writings and theatrical productions. Not surprisingly, given these two very different ways of looking at the play, from its first performance it has provoked controversy and extreme reactions.

The furore which greeted the first performance of *The Government Inspector* was summed up by Prince Vyazemsky in a postscript added in 1876 to his article first published in Pushkin's journal *The Contemporary* in 1836:

> The comedy was considered by many people to be a liberal declaration rather like Beaumarchais' comedy *The Barber of Seville*; it was seen as a kind of political fire-bomb that had been lobbed at society in the guise of a comedy. Some welcomed it and rejoiced in it as a bold, albeit disguised attack on the powers that be. In their view, Gogol, although choosing a district town as his field of battle, was aiming higher . . . Others, of course, looked upon the comedy as an attack on the state: they were alarmed and frightened by it and saw the unfortunate or fortunate comic writer almost as a dangerous rebel.

Gogol made repeated attempts to answer the various

criticisms which were levelled at the play. He was most concerned to counter accusations that his play lacked social impact. In his short dramatic sketch entitled *Upon Leaving the Theatre after the Performance of a New Comedy*, written in 1836 and revised for publication in 1842, he has a Very Modestly Dressed Man arguing that the play, by exposing corrupt officials, will strengthen the trust of the people in their government. At the end of the sketch the character of the Author steps forward to counter the accusation that the play contains no decent or virtuous characters by identifying laughter as the one truly honest character (see p.xxv).

This consistent line runs through Gogol's own writings about his play, namely that he intended to use laughter to expose society's ills as he saw them, not as light relief for a dilettante audience. As his epigraph to the play announces, 'Don't blame the mirror if your face is lopsided' and, as the Mayor says when he rounds on the audience, 'What do you think you're laughing at, eh?! You're laughing at yourselves, do you know that?' (p.95), the potential of comedy to reveal our own imperfections is firmly embedded in the playwright's objectives. As the process of revision of the text proceeded, largely provoked by the failure, in Gogol's eyes, of the 1836 production to fulfil his intentions accurately, Gogol deliberately removed many of the farcical, vaudeville elements and increased the satirical content. The 1842 version, on which all modern translations and productions are based, embodies his attacks on the corruption and bribery endemic in Russian bureaucracy. It can be said that Gogol's preoccupation was, through laughter, to persuade state officials to behave honestly and without hypocrisy.

In setting his play Gogol created a complete society in the inhabitants of his isolated country town. The characters represent a wide spectrum of contemporary Russian society – the peasants like Ossip and Mishka, the Mayor's servant, the poorer townspeople like the widow the Mayor has just had beaten, the merchants from whom the Mayor extorts

bribes, landowners in the shape of Bobchinsky and
Dobchinsky, lower-ranking provincial functionaries like the
police and middle-ranking officials like the Mayor. Gogol
also made no attempt to suggest that the corruption
evident in all the townspeople was different from the rest
of society. This gave rise to one of the key attacks on the
play – that there are no 'good' or 'honest' characters for
the audience to identify with. To attack the play on this
basis is obviously to ignore Gogol's prime purpose,
reflected in his deliberate move away from the conventions
of comedy at the time, which provided an optimistic
interpretation of life that would comfort and entertain the
audience. When the Mayor rounds on the audience to tell
them that they are only laughing at themselves Gogol's
message cannot be clearer; this comedy is designed to
make us think and change our behaviour and attitudes.
Gogol, in his *Selected Passages*, singled out social comedies
like Griboyedov's *Woe from Wit* as genuine because they
did not present a 'light-hearted mockery of the absurd
aspects of society' but exposed its 'wounds and diseases, its
grave internal abuses with the ruthless power of irony'.

The message is clear, the satire powerful and yet Gogol's
1846 claims for the symbolic import have also proved
deeply attractive to critics and theatre practitioners alike. In
making these claims for his play Gogol may have been
echoing an approach suggested by Belinsky, the influential
Russian critic whose championing of Gogol's play certainly
helped to establish its reputation and who described
Khlyestakov as 'the phantom shadow of the Mayor's guilty
conscience'. In 1906, about fifty years after Gogol's death,
the critic Merezhkovsky wrote an article entitled 'Gogol
and the Devil', which seems to have provided a platform
for interpretations of the play which emphasise the
symbolic at the expense of the satiric themes of the play.
For such critics, the fog which Zemlyanika refers to seems
to envelop the play and cloud the characters' judgements –
often as an emanation of evil, with Khlyestakov cast in the
role of the Devil, a devil of banal pettiness.

Nabokov, entitling his chapter on the play 'The Government Specter', describes the characters as 'nightmare people in one of those dreams when you think you have waked up while all you have done is to enter the most dreadful (most dreadful in its sham reality) region of dreams' (1961, p.42). However, he sees the play as both a social satire, which he calls 'the public view', and as a moral one, with 'Gogol's belated amendment' as essentially incorrect, since in his view:

> The characters of *The Government Inspector*, whether subject or not to imitation by flesh and blood, were true only in the sense that they were the true creatures of Gogol's fancy. (Ibid., p.41)

As for the immediate theatrical impact of the play, much of the controversy rested on the interpretation of the effect produced by the final tableau. As Gogol pointed out in his Notes (pp.6–7):

> The cast should be specially attentive to the concluding tableau. The final speech, from the Gendarme, must stun everybody on stage, immediately and simultaneously, like an electric shock. The entire company should shift and freeze its position in a single instant. An exclamation of astonishment must be given by all the female characters simultaneously, as it were from a single pair of lungs. If this business is not properly performed the whole effect may be ruined.

Gogol's apparent intention was to indicate that the power of the state in the shape of the newly arrived real Government Inspector would now put a stop to the bribery and corruption. The problem for the audience is that the strength and depth of the corrupt attitudes have been so securely established that it is easier to envisage the townspeople and particularly the officials recovering their façades and simply suborning the real Inspector. They are certainly not seen to be punished or robbed of their misappropriated advantages but simply exposed to ridicule. Despite all of Gogol's attempts to explain his motives, once his play was performed and in the public arena, political intentions would be ascribed to it which are often quite alien to the author himself.

The play in production

The first performance of the play was given at the Aleksandrinsky Theatre in St Petersburg on 19 April 1836. Following difficulties with the censor, the play's performance was authorised by the Tsar himself, Nicholas I, who also attended the first night accompanied by the Crown Prince (later Aleksandr II). Gogol was in the audience sharing a box with some literary friends and acquaintances. The Tsar was seen to enjoy the performance, laughing and applauding frequently, and is reported to have said afterwards, 'That was some play! Everyone received their come-uppance; and me most of all.' Gogol himself was far less happy, largely because a play which needed to be played in a certain comic style in order to bring out its satirical import, had been compromised by an approach which bordered on that of farce or vaudeville. It was partly in order to avoid a repetition of this that he set about revising the play between the publication of its first version, in 1836, and the rather different version which has come down to us, published in 1842.

The production had been preceded by a first reading given at the home of the poet Vasili Zhukovsky, on 18 January 1836, in the presence of Pushkin and others. In Russia, it is not unusual for the dramatist to read his own work, taking all the parts, and on this occasion Gogol's brilliant reading elicited much laughter and general praise. He arranged a further reading of the play for the benefit of the cast, which was held in the apartment of the man who was the first interpreter of the role of the Mayor, Ivan Sosnitsky. The actors were left feeling rather bemused, as well as shocked, by the realistic nature of the language, especially that of Ossip and the locksmith's wife. Gogol had cause for concern; not only did the actors seem unhappy with taking on the roles of corrupt officials and characters from low-life, but responsibility for the production had been placed in the hands of a bureaucratic administrator, A.I. Khrapovitsky. Gogol attended rehearsals and attempted to give the actors advice as to how their roles were to be interpreted but, with the exception of Sosnitsky, they tended to ignore him and go their own way. The role of Khlyestakov, as played by N.O. Diur, was especially out of keeping with Gogol's conception of the character, so much so that Gogol held out little hope for the play's success in performance.

The play's reception on the first night was a mixed one, partly because of uncertainty as to what kind of play this was, but, on the whole, the audience seemed determined to view it as a farce with slanderous implications (see Sergei Bertensson, 'The Première of *The Inspector General*' in N.V. Gogol, *The Inspector General*, ed. Henry Popkin, New York, Avon Books, 1976). The author was called for at the end as a matter of course, but Gogol had already left the theatre and did not appear on stage, which also gave offence. Subsequent performances were more warmly received but, as far as Gogol was concerned, the damage had been done. The play which he had intended as a moral critique of social evils had been acted in such a way that it offended both author and critics alike, albeit for different reasons. Some regarded the play as a farce characterised by a trivial plot and a well-worn theme, while the portrayal of the women seemed morally offensive. Others considered the fact that there were no morally positive characters in the play an insult to all Russian provincial towns. The language of the play was crude, even vulgar, and the comedy devoid of social significance. Some even suggested how the play could be improved by introducing 'good' characters to balance the 'bad' and advocated the introduction of a light romantic element to leaven the overall coarseness.

The one positive voice was that of a Prince Vyazemsky, who had attended the first reading and who recognised how important the play was, placing it in the main Russian comic tradition of Fonvizin and Griboyedov. He identified the thematic importance of the part played by 'fear', which justified what others saw as the implausibilities of the plotting, and pointed to the appropriateness of the language with its basis in characters who, if slightly caricatured, nevertheless had their roots in real life. This was too much for the likes of a fellow prince, Tsitsianov, who hurriedly wrote a riposte in the shape of a play called *The Real Government Inspector*, published in July 1836, in which it transpired that the real government inspector had been in town all along keeping an eye on things. At the end, he punished the officials, sent Khlyestakov into the army and married the Mayor's daughter.

The Moscow première, on 25 May, fared little better in terms of performance and reception, despite an interpretation of the Mayor by Mikhail Shchepkin which was far more in keeping with Gogol's idea of the role. A certain Count Fedor Tolstoy declared Gogol to be an enemy of Russia who should be clapped in irons and sent to Siberia although, generally, reviews in the Moscow press were more favourable than those in St Petersburg. V. Androsov in the *Moscow Observer* detected 'the inner truth of the Idea' in the play, which had the effect of placing it high among the small number of truly original dramas. In laughing at figures of authority Gogol was not mocking Authority itself, or Justice, but perversions of those same things. Gogol expressed his sense of hurt at the main brunt of the criticism to Shchepkin, 'Now I see what it means to be a comedy writer . . . I am appalled by the obtuse irritability which pervades all classes of our society . . . To call a crook a crook is to undermine the foundations of our State' (letter of 29 April 1836). Everyone was against him, he said, the police, the merchants as well as the literary people. Two months after the première, he fled abroad.

The first performance of the revised 1842 text was at the Aleksandrinsky Theatre, in 1870. Where one of Gogol's

complaints in 1836 had related to the exaggerated and
inappropriate costuming, an attempt was now made to
dress the play in the appropriate style of the 1830s. The
director, Yablochkin, had been influenced by the taste for
'archaeological naturalism' in European theatre, whereby a
production, in order to demonstrate serious intent, sought
to be faithful less to the text than to the milieu in which
the play was set.

The centenary of Gogol's birth was celebrated during
the 1908/9 season and was marked in Russia by a number
of productions of *The Government Inspector*, none more
important than the one staged by Stanislavky at the
Moscow Art Theatre. It, too, was conceived in
'archaeologically naturalistic' style and a great deal of time
and attention were devoted to achieving an impression of
complete authenticity and verisimilitude. Every samovar,
teaspoon and ornament was selected to correspond to the
period of the 1830s. On this very realistic foundation,
however, Stanislavsky constructed an almost abstract
version of the play. The curtain rose on a group of
monstrous grotesques who moved in slow and stylised
fashion, emphasising their words with strangely sibilant
whistles and hisses. Against this background, Khlyestakov
and Ossip appeared lively and more human. The overall
impression, according to one critic, was like observing
events through a giant magnifying glass.

Stanislavsky directed the play again, in 1921, as a
phantasmagoria of mass-psychosis in tragi-comic grotesque
style, as a whole town came under the spell of the 'petty
demon' of a travelling clerk (a reference to a recent
symbolist novel by Fiodor Sologub called *The Petty
Demon*). The production was chiefly memorable for the
virtuoso performance of Khlyestakov given by Anton
Chekhov's nephew, Michael Chekhov (who later emigrated
and founded a drama studio at Dartington Hall, Devon, in
the late 1930s). The tradition which had characterised the
role up to this point was one which saw Khlyestakov as a
superficial dandy and mannered cosmopolitan, rather than

the feather-brained improviser whom Gogol describes.
Michael Chekhov turned him into a complete nonentity,
devoid of any gifts or talent whatsoever. Before his
confrontation at the inn with the bear-like figure of the
Mayor, played by Ivan Moskvin, Chekhov cowered behind
the door whimpering like a frightened child.

The strength of Chekhov's performance lay in the way
in which this nonentity became transformed into a
'somebody'; of terrifying consequence – into an image
which, according to some, assumed psychopathological
dimensions. Under the influence of his suddenly-acquired
grandeur, Chekhov's Khlyestakov developed into a being
both psychotic and fiendish. Anything seemed possible and
every fantastic untruth became a potential truth, without
any loss of psychological plausibility. He seemed to lead a
life of mythological proportions in which each of his words
and every one of his actions became the potential subject
of legend. When, for example, describing the 700-rouble
melon, this Khlyestakov even had the outrageous
confidence to outline a *square* one in the air with his
finger, a figment to which everyone on stage responded by
nodding in eager and awestruck recognition.

Post-revolutionary productions of the play included
versions 'for Red Army men, sailors and workers', staged
in 1919, in which bourgeois bad taste was suggested by the
pink décor of the Mayor's front parlour which also
contained a canary. A three-act version by D. Smolin,
called *Comrade Khlyestakov* was staged at the Theatre of
Drama and Comedy, Moscow, in 1922, which apart from
reducing the play considerably tried to bring it up-to-date
by interpolating poems by the communist poet, Vladimir
Mayakovsky. A production at the Moscow Trades Union
Theatre in 1925 mixed constructivist scenery with authentic
antiquarian objects. General anarchy is said to have
reigned on stage, where group scenes were played in
stylised, grotesque fashion, while individual roles were
acted realistically. This production was staged by Valeri
Bebutov, a former colleague of Vsevolod Meyerhold. In

1926, the latter staged what is undoubtedly the most famous production of the play to date, but one which had to wait until the 1970s to achieve wide recognition.

Meyerhold's plans for staging the play had been formulated some twenty years previously when he first read an essay by the Russian Symbolist, Dmitri Merezhkovsky, called 'Gogol and the Devil'. The production united elements of *commedia dell'arte*, symbolist and expressionist motifs, pantomime, harlequinade, techniques of oriental theatre, bio-mechanics, opera and ballet. It was staged with minute exactitude and ran almost throughout to musical accompaniment. As self-styled 'author of the production', Meyerhold broke the five-act play down into fifteen scenes, each with its own title, wrote in lines and characters from Gogol's earlier versions of the play and borrowed themes and characters from Gogol's other work. A particular, and notorious, instance was the role of a travelling officer in uniform who, like a mysterious *doppelgänger*, accompanied Khlyestakov throughout, his alien presence constituting a mute comment on the progress of the action. (For a reconstruction of the production as a whole, see Nick Worrall, 'Meyerhold Directs Gogol's *Government Inspector*', *Theatre Quarterly* 2, no.7, 1972, pp.75–95.)

The central figure of Khlyestakov was strangely garbed and contemplated the world through a pair of square, horn-rimmed spectacles, looking now like a malignant undertaker, now like a skittish mandarin, next like a pathetic child, in a process of endless transformations. The production became a series of *tours de force* utilising the minimal resources of a truck-stage of narrow dimensions which ran on rails from the rear to the front of the stage for some of the scenes. Otherwise, the whole width of the stage was used, on which an arc of polished mahogany doors gleamed as a reflection of the extravagant luxury of an epoch and a location transferred, for Meyerhold's purposes, from Gogol's Russian backwoods to a town resembling the capital itself. The bribe scenes, instead of being separate episodes, were staged as a single

nightmarish dream of universal corruption as a
somnambulistic Khlyestakov drifted across the stage
relieving disembodied hands of packages of money as these
were poked through a crack in each of the doors which
encircled the stage.

If Meyerhold's production is the most famous, the claim
for the most outrageous was that staged by Igor Terentiev,
in Leningrad in 1927. Much influenced by the so-called
'Eccentric' movement, actors crawled about the stage and
interpolated into the dialogue quotations from Freud and
chunks of Polish and Ukrainian. The approach was openly
scatalogical, undoubtedly influenced by a Soviet critic's
Freudian theory that Gogol had sexual problems and an
anal fixation. Clutching rolls of toilet paper, each character
fought at every other moment to get to a lavatory set in
the centre of the stage. The Mayor spent most of his time
on all fours, explosions were detonated during the action
and live mice were released on stage. Costumes were of
cubist design with motifs suggestive of each official's trade
emblazoned on them – a skull on his sleeve for the
Doctor, postage stamps and envelopes on the Postmaster's
trousers and strawberry designs on the Charity
Commissioner's backside. To the strains of Beethoven's
Moonlight Sonata, Khlyestakov went to the toilet clutching
a candle while the Mayor conducted an entire scene
ensconced on the lavatory, registering his efforts in the
tones of his voice. In the wooing scene, Khlyestakov
disappeared into the lavatory with the Mayor's daughter
where they were observed by the Mayor through the
keyhole. At another point, the locksmith's wife was taken
off behind a divan by Ossip, where it soon became
apparent that 'relations' were taking place. At the end, the
real Government Inspector turned out to have been
Khlyestakov all along.

In 1966, a former actor at the Meyerhold Theatre, Igor
Ilinsky, staged a production at the Moscow Maly Theatre,
which made great use of the mirror image contained in the
play's epigraph, 'Don't blame the mirror if your face is

lopsided'. This folk saying was broadcast over loudspeakers before curtain-rise, the curtain itself taking the form of a mirror in which the audience could see itself. This effect was then amplified by distorting mirrors which formed part of each setting and the final tableau was ingeniously contrived to last the full minute and a half which Gogol asks for.

In the West, Gogol is best known as the author of *Dead Souls* and the *Petersburg Tales*, and his plays, with the exception of *The Government Inspector*, are little-known and rarely performed. The play's first performance in Britain was in June 1906 by the Stage Society at the Scala Theatre, London, in a three-act version.

However, the first significant staging in London was that by the émigré Russian director Theodore Komisarjevsky at the Duke of York's Theatre, in 1920. A revival at the Barnes Theatre in 1926 of this same production, but with Charles Laughton as Ossip and Claude Rains as Khlyestakov, suggests that a more straightforward version of the play in 1920 had been replaced by something rather more stylised:

> Mr Kommissarjevski's production . . . leaves one gasping; for he has turned an early Victorian farce into a cubist ballet . . . If you are going to take such liberties with the spirit of an author . . . it may become necessary to rewrite the play as well as advertise the whole as a ballet on a theme of Gogol. But nothing can hide the fact that *The Inspector General* provides an admirable entertainment . . . this amazing producer has brought off [a] *tour de force*. (Victor Borovsky, *A Triptych from the Russian Theatre: The Komossarzhevskys*, London, Hurst & Co., 2001, p.368)

The next production was staged by John Fernald at the Arts Theatre, London, during the 1940s, in a version by Guy McCrone, with Geoffrey Dunn and Morris Sweden as Khlyestakov and the Mayor, played respectively as shiftless ne'er-do-well and minor bureaucrat. While the timing and pace were appropriate it all seemed rather too reminiscent of an English comedy of manners, with the result that the

undertone of social criticism and the play's satirical sting
were missing. The final appearance of the real Government
Inspector, in this context, seemed anti-climactic.

The first major production on the West End stage was
that staged by John Burrell at the New Theatre, London,
in February 1948, in a translation by D.G. Campbell,
designed by Felix Topolski and with Alec Guinness,
Bernard Miles and Harry Andrews as Khlyestakov, the
Mayor and Ossip. According to one observer, the
production saw the characters as 'eccentrics in the true
Dickens tradition' but emphasised that 'they are *eccentrics*,
not caricatures' – a fact about which Gogol 'left
incontrovertible advice' when he stated that 'The main
thing to guard against is caricature'.

Regrettably the production tended to ignore Gogol's
advice. According to Audrey Williamson, it 'blew the
whole comedy into the contours of a charade, like a
monstrous balloon'. The production's excesses included a
scene in which the shopkeepers were made to kneel with
their faces on the floor chanting their complaints mock-
liturgically while Khlyestakov chanted back like a priest.
The notable exception was Guinness, who

> gave a performance absolutely in accord with Gogol's own
> instructions on the art of comedy acting . . . Serious to the core,
> slyly enjoying the joke as the *character* . . . would enjoy it, playing
> a scene of inebriation with supreme delicacy of touch, he
> succeeded in holding his own effortlessly in comic effect with any
> grotesque on the stage, and gave the performance a note of artistic
> distinction it would not otherwise have enjoyed. (Audrey
> Williamson, *Old Vic Drama 2, 1947–1957*, London, Rockliff, 1957,
> pp.8–10)

Bernard Miles as a 'rubicundly corrupt Mayor [was]
engagingly and deceptively simple', while the rest of the
cast (which included Kenneth Connor, Mark Dignam and
Renee Asherson) 'went for the characters with a joyous
ferocity in a flamboyant set of make-ups'. In general, 'these
prancing babies were as disarming, and lacking in venom

as Mr Micawber, and the faint sociological voice of Nikolai Gogol broke disturbingly through. "In *The Government Inspector* I tried to gather in a heap all that was bad in Russia. I wished to turn it all into ridicule'" (ibid.).

Preparing his production at the Aldwych Theatre, London, in 1966, which featured Paul Scofield, Paul Rogers, David Warner and Patience Collier and for which the present translation was commissioned, Peter Hall addressed his cast as follows:

> 'The first thing that needs to be said about the play is that we must approach it first and foremost absolutely with straight faces . . . with the most utter seriousness.' The actors needed to work on it, 'as if we were doing a play of Chekhov's', but with a sense that, 'normality is excessively abnormal', where 'the true meaning of the surreal is surreality . . . a bit larger than life', but not 'consciously funny, consciously grotesque'. (Peter Hall, 'Talking to the Cast' in *The Inspector General*, ed. Henry Popkin, New York, Avon Books, 1976, pp.146–54)

However, reviewing the production, Mary Holland described it as:

> Peter Hall country where the stage gets filled with clumping yokels, rosy cheeks, would-be gentry, Egg Marketing Board voices, theatrical business, sides of ham, home-made liquor and human frailty . . . There is more to the play that this gusty, broad-beamed farce [which] is lovely as far as it goes – but it doesn't go anywhere . . . And so the stage is set for Scofield – mincing, lean-shanked, beautiful in his lime-green frock-coat, ashblond curls and alabaster smooth face just cracking a little at the edges. He speaks with [a] mixture of accents merged into an irresistible voice – part suppressed cockney, part artistic queer, part the dead flatness of the Whisky Priest. His timing is more daring than a Whitehall veteran's; he splits his sentences unpredictably with a helpless wave of his hands, as though incapable of following one train of thought long enough to complete the second half of a sentence when he plunges confidently into the first . . . It is easy to believe that he takes too long to cotton on to what is happening, that his boasting rings nearly true in his own ears, that he becomes more and more

fluent as his audience warms to him and he to them. In short,
Scofield gives us a believable human being as well as a prodigious
display of technique. The production as a whole is merely a
prodigious display. (*Plays and Players*, March 1966, pp.16–19)

The production had been influenced by the Moscow Art
Theatre dramatisation of Gogol's *Dead Souls* seen as part
of the World Theatre Season at the Aldwych in 1964.
According to Michael Billington, 'The caricatures were not
as carefully individualised as in the Moscow Arts
production but . . . still had a rich comic texture; in
particular the drunk scene, with hordes of people squeezed
into a single room, and tripping endlessly over each other's
feet' (*The Modern Actor*, London, Hamish Hamilton, 1973,
pp.51–2).

The Marsh and Brooks translation was used by Toby
Robertson for his revival of *The Government Inspector* at the
Old Vic Theatre, London, in 1979, with Ian Richardson,
Hugh Sullivan and Barbara Jefford. The production
showed the influence of both Meyerhold's 1926 version
and one staged by Georgi Tovstonogov at the Bolshoi
Drama Theatre, Leningrad, in 1972. Prior to the arrival of
Khlyestakov at the Mayor's house, Meyerhold had
imagined a fantasy sequence in which the Mayor's wife has
visions of being paid court to by a whole group of dashing
army officers who serenade her, present her with bouquets
of flowers and, in one instance of an officer whose
advances she spurns, commit suicide. Robertson staged a
similar scene as well as borrowing a device from the
Tovstonogov production which had the Government
Inspector's carriage suspended threateningly over the heads
of the protagonists, with its wheels activated into
movement whenever fear of authority gripped the
townsfolk.

Probably the most ambitious British production of the
play was the one staged at the National Theatre, in 1985,
directed by Richard Eyre, with Rik Mayall as Khlyestakov.
Eyre had staged the play eleven years previously at the
Nottingham Playhouse with an anglicised Yorkshire setting

of post-war austerity where black marketeering was a
feature of English, rather than Russian, life. Now, Eyre
detected a very serious, dark side to the play which dealt
with 'a ghastly world where people are living constantly in
fear of the jackboot; it's about how people behave under
the threat of a police state'. Using a version by Adrian
Mitchell, Eyre took a further leaf out of Meyerhold's book
by introducing scenes from other Gogol works, in this case
Dead Souls, and employing the scenic device of a truck-
stage. In an interview, Eyre described the play as a
microcosm of

> a whole world where fear is the dominant emotion and where
> behaviour is predicated on the assumption that somebody is
> listening behind your left shoulder. Such insane behaviour is only
> possible in a world that is objectively insane – insane in the way
> that all autocracies and totalitarian states are objectively insane.
> The worlds of Stalin and Hitler were insane by any objective
> standards. So I wanted to do justice to Gogol's vision of an insane
> world. ('In Search of the Real Gogol', *Plays*, March 1985,
> pp.14–17)

In the event, the production seemed to be swamped by
over-ambition, characterised by a dominant backcloth
which depicted a 'landscape of snow and steppes, a sea of
giant magnified documents, yellowing ledgers, huge
bluebottles, ink pots and writing implements which
submerge[d] the stage and dominate[d] town hall, inn and
governor's home which are tucked in as needed' (Giles
Gordon, *Punch*, 13 February 1985). The production was
'punctuated by snowstorms and thunderclaps, the crash of
falling masonry, and crunch of broken glass [ending] with
Khlyestakov soaring upwards to the sky in some sort of
secular apotheosis on a massive fork-lift troika'. What
seemed to have happened was 'that Gogol's savage, dream-
like satire has somehow acclimatised itself to an equally
authentic but much milder type of English nursery
surrealism' where

> Rik Mayall plays Khlyestakov as a cross between Mad Hatter and

March Hare with a touch of the White Rabbit's self-importance and florid condescension; white-faced, wild-eyed, thick-skinned, crack-brained, with a mane of boisterous, upstanding electrically eccentric hair and hands so expressive that, at one point, he manages to upstage a fellow actor from behind the scenes with nothing but two fingers poking through two holes. The effect is startling, scurrilous, absurd but entirely harmless. . . . [Eyre's] production will be remembered for its spectacular staging, and . . . a cheerful philosophy that wouldn't at bottom hurt a fly, let alone tamper with ancient, comfortable, theatrical conventions of nostalgia, complacency and standard sentiment. (Hilary Spurling, *Plays*, March 1985, p.24)

The production began with lightning, a torrent of stage mist and the transformation of a picture of Tsar Nicholas I into a ravening monster, and ended with yet more flashings and bangings. *À la* Meyerhold, it also introduced a fantasy sequence, in which elegant dancers acted out the imposter Khlyestakov's yearnings for success in the Petersburg ballrooms. In the words of Benedict Nightingale, the 'production [was] not so much Meyerhold as Meyerhalved . . . Meyerhold's *Government Inspector*, some said was too "mystical" . . . Accordingly, Eyre [gave] special emphasis to the scene in which merchants, women and other abused citizens come to complain about the Mayor's injustices . . . stretching out their importunate hands to soulful chords from Dominic Muldowney's score' (*New Statesman*, 8 February 1985). The loud noises at beginning and end were doubtless prompted by Nabokov's observation that the action of the play occurs between a flash of lightning (the play's minatory opening) and the subsequent thunderclap (the appearance of the Gendarme at the end). Ned Chaillet detected some of the more serious connotations which Eyre's conception of the play imagined, especially during the lying scene when Rik Mayall, 'soar[ed] into a speech that strikes the townspeople with fear, trembling and admiration . . . At the height of his fantasy, with an audience that Hitler would have envied, he smashe[d] the bust of the mayor and climb[ed] on to the plinth to cheers' (*Wall Street Journal*, 8 February 1985).

A touring production by Don Taylor in 1988, with Anthony Quayle as the Mayor and Paul Rhys as Khlyestakov, seemed to lack any clear governing idea but was rescued by actors who played the townsfolk as

> a ramshackle crew of posers and hangers-on, stuffed out with pomp and circumstance, strutting or decrepit, up to their glazed eyes in gullibility. Timothy Bateson's frock-coated and vacuous schools superintendant, tottering towards senility, Wolfe Morris's charity commissioner, stuffed out like a turkey and exuding chronic self-importance, John Woodnut's Judge, furtive as a shoplifter, and Philip Manikum's gabbling landowner, in the first flush of juicy gossip, all manage to avoid the pitfalls of grotesque playing and beautifully evoke the play's lurid comedy. So too does Sir Anthony Quayle, at 75 heroically leading his company all over the country . . . He is an ideal foil to Paul Rhys's government inspector [who] plays the imposter as a childlike fantasist, lost in a world of wounded and querulous hauteur. (Nicholas de Jongh, *Guardian*, 13 May 1988)

In January 1989, the Anglo-Asian Tara Arts Group staged an Indian-English adaptation of the play by Anuradha Kapur as *Ala Afsur*, relocating the play

> in an India still dominated by memories of the Raj . . . Burlesquing the wiles of petty officials in the mouldering depths of a vast empire, the play adapts happily to its transfer to the subcontinent. Characters now travel in tongas, not droshkies. Tiffin is taken instead of vodka. Mangoes and masala replace cabbage soup and sturgeon . . . The babu boobies parodied in this play never stop chattering about 'Blighty'. To be 'Blighty returned' is the ultimate aspiration. The imposter tightens his hold on the anxieties, purses and womenfolk of the quailing locals by conversing about his palatial quarters in 'Regent Circus', his easy familiarity with 'the memsahibs of Soho Square' and his authorship of such famous West End plays as *The Mouse in the Trap* . . . The cast . . . handsomely costumed in Mogul tunics, velvet trousers and vividly-sashed blouses have their faces decorated with the

coloured stripes and patterns of Indian theatre. There are chants,
somersaultings, a dream sequence resembling a folklore demon-
drama, and an interlude that seems like something from a
romantic Hindu film. (Peter Kemp, *Independent*, 23 January 1989)

The Katona Jozsef Theatre from Budapest brought their
production of *The Government Inspector* to London in July
1989, where it played at the Old Vic Theatre in repertory
with a production of Chekhov's *Three Sisters*, both in
Hungarian. The production seemed to many to make a
powerful statement about Eastern European existence
under post-Stalinist rule. The first scene established the
tone, set in a committee room of 'unwashed battleship
grey lockers [with] a leaking roof, a recalcitrant slow-speed
fan, [and] a collection of party deadbeats clad in the usual
Karl Marx C&A tat; a police chief in a stupid uniform, a
snakelike bureaucrat clad in a mountainous woolly, [and]
someone with a shorty black-leather coat and shades'
(Steve Grant, *Time Out*, 19 July 1989). The production
appeared to be set 'less in provincial Russia than in some
mildewed modern satellite . . . putrescent with images of
decay: a grey canvas roof pocked with holes, a line of
rusting metal lockers that serve for exits and entrances, a
batch of pigeon-holes obviously filled with dead letters, a
skew-whiff baroque lift apparently stuck for eternity
between floors' (Michael Billington, *Guardian*, 15 July
1989). Janos Ban played Khlyestakov

> as a total nonentity who simply cannot believe his luck . . . a
> complete klutz who even in his seedy hotel room gets his spidery
> frame caught up in a collapsible bed [and in the lying scene] finds
> himself clinging precariously to a hoistable clothes-horse and
> reaching desperately for the drink he has placed on a rotating fan
> . . . When Peter Blasko's harassed Governor enters to find
> Khlyestakov noisily rutting with his spreadeagled wife, he is too
> preoccupied with complaints levelled at him by tradesmen to care
> about being cuckolded . . . This is a world in which everything
> from personal integrity to one's wife and daughter are up for sale.
> (Ibid.)

A production by Matthew Francis at the Greenwich
Theatre in April 1991 was most notable for its setting – 'a
steeply raked ramshackle revolve that spins round like a
fairground icon of Mother Russia to some catchy balalaika
numbers'. Timothy Spall's Khlyestakov was 'a preening
infant, forever twisting his hair in knots and stuffing
himself with money like chocolate bars'. The town officials
were 'a harmless group of Toytown grotesques' (Irving
Wardle, *Independent on Sunday*). The production, which
opened with a scene in which the Mayor was seen stuffing
potentially incriminating documents into an incinerator,
seemed to dwell on physical squalor with the lower halves
of the town inhabitants 'bespattered with mud, replenished
from a miniature quagmire at the front of the stage.
Scenes open to an accompaniment of farmyard noises.
Stuffed goats and poultry and what looks like a dead
peasant adorn the ramshackle revolving onion-domed set
which serves as government office, inn and mayor's
residence' (Lindsey Hughes, *Times Literary Supplement*, 3
May 1991). Timothy Spall's Khlyestakov was a
combination of Kenneth Williams, Max Wall and Maurice
Chevalier, 'in a highly entertaining performance which is
strong on knock-about, slightly camp humour, but light on
the menace which underlies Khlyestakov's function in the
play. The predominant red of the sets hints at his
"devilish" nature, but may equally allude to the "regal
colour" of the Court of the characters' imaginings' (ibid.).
Ronald Eyre's version of the play had Khlyestakov quoting
from *The Rime of the Ancient Mariner* and 'The Boy Stood
on the Burning Deck' and a line during the lying scene, 'I
have enormous balls', got a laugh through deliberate
distortion of the original text.

In 1994, Dubbeljoint Productions, so called because
based jointly in Dublin and Belfast, brought their
production of Marie Jones's Irish adaptation of the play to
London for a short season at Kilburn's Tricycle Theatre.
The action was advanced to the turn of the twentieth
century and Gogol's world became an Ulster outpost of

the Protestant Ascendancy with Catholic peasants instead
of serfs and with London replacing St Petersburg. The
officials became inhabitants of an isolated Northern Irish
border town where 'eminent fraudsters . . . live in fear of
an inspector from "the mainland". Local scams include
evicting religiously incorrect tenants and using the recently
vacated land for illegal cattle dealings. When a nomadic
layabout son of an Anglo-Irish landlord breezes through,
his west British accent fools the local community' (John
O'Mahoney, 'The Power and the Paranoia', *Guardian*, 3
February 1994). According to the director, Pam Brighton,
it was a play about people who feel remote from the
centres of power. 'This results in incredible levels of
corruption running hand in hand with animosity. It's a
terrible sense of inferiority' (ibid.). Instead of the Mayor's
parlour, the play opened in an abattoir hung with
enormous carcasses among which the officials played a
game of hide-and-seek. Dan Gordon's Khlyestakov recited
chunks from Yeats and Brian Merriman's *The Midnight
Court* during the lying scene. The physical comedy of the
production was both vigorous and hilarious, 'achieving one
poteen-crazed, crotch-nuzzling climax at the mayoral party,
and topping it with another in the bribery scene, where
Gordon holds court in bed to a queue of palm-greasing
worthies while pleasuring the mayor's wife under the
sheets' (Irving Wardle, *Independent on Sunday*, 6 February
1994).

Possibly aware of the way in which the play can
successfully be transferred to a regional milieu with
appropriate dialect and accent, Paisley-born dramatist John
Byrne's adaptation was staged at the Almeida Theatre,
London, in December 1997, directed by Jonathan Kent
and with Ian McDiarmid as the Mayor and Tom
Hollander as Khlyestakov. In this Russo-Scottish hybrid,
the Mayor became the Lord Provost (while still riding in a
'droshky') and 'smokies' co-existed with samovars. The
production was set in what looked like the remains of a
house which had just exploded, perched on a rubbish heap

lxii THE GOVERNMENT INSPECTOR

of paper and junk, with splintered walls and sagging floors. The acting seemed to border on the manic with the notable exception of Tom Hollander, whose 'marvellous performance' justified the evening:

> with his pouting features and reddish Brillo-pad hair [and] look of a savage infant. Left on his own, he executes dainty little twirls in front of the mirror. [When being flattered] he enters a realm of capricious fantasy claiming, at one point, to have written *The Marriage of Figaro*, *Robinson Crusoe* and *The Three Musketeers* . . . When he asks, in bewilderment, 'Who do they think I am?' it is as if he himself is struggling to resolve his own identity. (Michael Billington, *Guardian*, 5 December 1997)

For John Peter, Hollander's performance was that of 'a Bertie Wooster of the steppes', an 'imperious little nincompoop' who gave

> a hilarious, beautifully accomplished and intelligent account of inspired and smug stupidity . . . Add to this the dimwitted confidence of a spoilt young toff and you get an irresistibly funny comedy of panic, petulant indignation and the survival of the unfittest [in a play where] everybody reacts like Pavlov's dogs, and you realise that Gogol has dramatised the claustrophobic world of conditioned reflexes. (*Sunday Times*, 28 December 1997)

Since the 1950s, there have been productions by Joan Littlewood's Theatre Workshop in 1953, a televised version starring the comedian Tony Hancock in 1958, as well as radio and theatre adaptations set in the North of England, Scotland, Wales and Ireland. Given that Gogol was a Ukrainian, regional versions of the play may perhaps be said to correspond best to the kind of world Gogol depicts. As far as the play's language is concerned, Vladimir Nabokov stated that it would take an Irishman to capture, in English, the authentic flavour of Gogol's Russian. There has also been a Hollywood film, staring Danny Kaye, in 1949, which set the play in a kind of Ruritania with songs, and called *The Inspector General*, a title the play is more commonly given in the United States.

Further Reading

Beresford, Michael, *Gogol's 'The Government Inspector'*,
London, Bristol Classical Press, 1997

Chekhov, Michael, 'A Play is Born: *The Government
Inspector'* in Charles Leonard (ed.), *Michael Chekhov's To
the Director and Playwright*, New York and Evanston,
Harper & Row, 1963

Gippius, Vasily, '*The Inspector General*: Structure and
Problems' in Robert A. Maguire (ed. and trans.), *Gogol
from the Twentieth Century*, New Jersey, Princeton
University Press, 1976

Gippius, V.V., *Gogol*, ed. and trans. Robert A. Maguire,
Durham and London, Duke University Press, 1989

Gogol, Nikolai, *Letters*, ed. Carl Proffer, trans. C. Proffer
and Vera Krivoshein, Ann Arbor, University of
Michigan, 1967

Gogol, Nikolai, *Selected Passages from Correspondence with
Friends*, trans. Jesse Zeldin, Nashville, Vanderbilt
University Press, 1969

Gogol, Nikolay, 'Gogol on the Theater and his Own Plays'
in Milton Ehre and Fruma Gottschalk (ed. and trans.),
The Theater of Nikolay Gogol: Plays and Selected Writings,
Chicago and London, University of Chicago Press, 1980

Gogol, Nikolai, *Hanz Kuechelgarten, Leaving the Theatre &
Other Works: Early Writings, Essays, Book Reviews &
Letters*, ed. Ronald Meyer, Ann Arbor, Ardis Publishers,
1990

Gogol, N.V., *Revizor (The Government Inspector)*, ed. W.
Harrison, London, Bradda Books and Oxford, Basil
Blackwell, 1964; reissued by Bristol Classical Press,
London, 1992

Gogol, N.V., *Revizor (The Government Inspector)*, *A
Comedy in Five Acts*, ed. M. Beresford, Studies in Slavic

Language and Literature, vol.9, Lewiston/Queenston/ Lampeter, Edwin Mellen Press, 1996

Gogol, Nikolai, *Three Plays: The Government Inspector, Marriage, The Gamblers*, trans. and intro. Stephen Mulrine, London, Methuen, 1999

Ivanov, Vyacheslav, 'Gogol's *Inspector General* and the Comedy of Aristophanes' in Robert A. Maguire (ed. and trans.), *Gogol from the Twentieth Century*, New Jersey, Princeton University Press, 1976

Karlinsky, Simon, *Russian Drama from its Beginnings to the Age of Pushkin*, Berkeley and London, University of California Press, 1985

Merezhkovsky, Dmitry, 'Gogol and the Devil' in Robert A. Maguire (ed. and trans.), *Gogol from the Twentieth Century*, New Jersey, Princeton University Press, 1976

Nabokov, Vladimir, *Nikolai Gogol*, New York, New Directions Publishing, 1961

Setchkarev, Vsevolod, *Gogol: His Life and Works*, trans. Robert Kramer, London, Peter Owen, 1965

Worrall, Nick, *Nikolai Gogol and Ivan Turgenev*, London and Basingstoke, Macmillan, 1982

THE GOVERNMENT INSPECTOR

an English version by
Edward O. Marsh and Jeremy Brooks

Don't blame the mirror if your
face is lopsided.
                    – *popular saying*

This version of *The Government Inspector* was prepared especially for the Royal Shakespeare Company's production at the Aldwych Theatre in January 1966. The play is set in a small provincial town in the heart of Russia, far from St Petersburg and Moscow. This distance from the capitals is important. As the Mayor says, 'You could gallop for three years without reaching a foreign country'. It is this sense of the vast distances between themselves and any centre of authority which gives the officials of Gogol's town a feeling of security from outside interference, and allows them to administer the town as corruptly and inefficiently as they like; and makes it inevitable that even the lowliest clerk from St Petersburg should seem, in their eyes, to glow with sophistication, wit and authority.

It is essential, therefore, that the speech of the officials and townspeople should have a distinctly provincial flavour, to contrast with the acquired polish which Khlyestakov has picked up in the capital. In order to avoid the inevitable 'Mummerset' which tends to emerge when actors are asked to produce an unspecified country accent, Peter Hall, the director, decided to imagine the play as being set in a remote East Anglian village. Suffolk and Norfolk are, in fact, not all that far from London, but they nevertheless do have a curious sense of remoteness from 'civilisation'; and the rhythms and vowel sounds of East Anglian speech are so distinctive that there seemed a fair chance of our being able to impose some cohesion on the accents used by the cast. We had a tape, made from BBC recordings, of East Anglian dialect stories, which was repeatedly played over to the cast during rehearsals; and expert coaching from two East Anglians – Donald Burton and Peter Hall.

This tape was also used in preparing the text. The starting point was Edward Marsh's original translation from the

Russian, which was then adapted as far as possible to fit the rhythms and speech patterns of our chosen dialect. In the case of the two visitors from the capital, we imagined Ossip as a cockney water-rat. Khlyestakov as a suburban dandy with pretensions above his station. This is not quite faithful to the Russian text, since both Khlyestakov and his servant originally came from a country province even more remote than the one they are now passing through; but it is not possible, in England, to 'place' them with the same social accuracy if they are also given a provincial accent.

The Russian custom, unfamiliar to our ears, of using the patronymic as well as the Christian name in ordinary conversation was to some extent made easier to deal with by contraction, so that 'Amos Fyodorovich' became 'Amos Fy'do'vich', and 'Artemy Philipovich' became 'Art'y Ph'lip'ich'. These contracted forms which do not necessarily correspond to actual Russian abbreviations, are given, in parentheses in the cast list, together with the adapted versions of some of the names which were used in this production. The justification for also changing many of the surnames – 'Lyapkin-Tyapkin' into 'Flapkin-Slapkin', 'Khlopov' into 'Plopov', is that most of Gogol's names have, in Russian, either a direct or an onomatopoeic joke-meaning. The civil ranks which we have attributed to the town's officials are a necessary invention. In nineteenth-century Russia, official society was divided into a seemingly infinite gradation of ranks – one of the proliferations of tsarist bureaucracy which Gogol was always attacking – but a direct transcript of these into English would be either meaningless or misleading.

Textual cuts which were found necessary for the Aldwych production in the course of rehearsals have been indicated by enclosing the cut passages in square brackets.

NOTES BY GOGOL
ON CHARACTERS AND COSTUMES

THE MAYOR. His hair has turned grey in the government service but in his way he is far from being a fool. He takes bribes but still manages to keep a certain measure of dignity. He is quite a serious person, something of a moralist, in fact. What he says is never too much, never too little; when he does speak it is never too loud, never too soft, and yet his every word is heavy with meaning. His features are as coarse and cruel as those of any successful person who has begun at the bottom in a difficult service. He veers rapidly from fear to joy, from subservience to arrogance, as befits a man with scarcely developed spiritual feelings. He is normally dressed in the frock-coat of his official uniform, of which the most striking features are the buttons and button-holes. In addition to this he wears spurred and highly-polished jack-boots. His hair is short and grizzled.

ANNA ANDREYEVNA, the Mayor's wife, is a provincial coquette, not exactly old yet, whose education has been about equally divided between romantic novels and anthology verse. Her main concerns are the pantry and the servants. She is extremely inquisitive and her vanity is displayed at every turn. She now and then gets the upper hand of her husband simply because he is not ready with an answer. She uses this power only for trivial things, however, lecturing him and sneering at him turn and turn about. She has four complete changes of costume during the play.

KHLYESTAKOV, a young man of twenty-three – slender, not to say thin. He tends to be rather silly, to the extent even, as the saying goes, of being 'not quite all there' – the sort of person his fellow workers in the same office consider a dead loss. He speaks and acts without a thought for anything or anybody. He is quite incapable of giving his undivided attention to any single idea. His speech is convulsive, the words jerk out in a totally unexpected fashion. The more simple and ingenuous the actor can appear in this part the better he will be. Khlyestakov dresses very fashionably.

OSSIP, Khlyestakov's servant, is rather like all servants who are getting on in years – serious in manner, eyes usually downcast, a moraliser given to treating himself to sermons he really means for his master. His voice is normally quite flat and smooth – though when talking to his master he can be rough and abrupt to the point of rudeness. He is more intelligent than his master and so he grasps things more rapidly, but he is not very willing to talk and, being a rascal into the bargain, prefers to keep his own counsel. He wears a long, grey or blue jacket, visibly threadbare.

BOBCHINSKY and DOBCHINSKY, two landowners, of the breed that would rather live in town than on their estates. Both are short and squat and very inquisitive. They are extraordinarily alike. They both chatter rather than speak, helping their words along with hand-waving and gesticulation. Dobchinsky is slightly the taller and more serious of the two, Bobchinsky jollier and livelier.

LYAPKIN-TYAPKIN, the Judge. A man who has read five or six books and who consequently inclines to freethinking. He is a great one for conjecture and as a result his every word has an air of profundity. The actor playing the part must keep a look of deep significance throughout and he must always speak in an exaggerated drawl, sounding rather like those grandfather clocks that strain and hiss before they strike.

ZEMLYANIKA, the Charity Commissioner, is a stout, clumsy, cumbersome man, who is nevertheless a wily rascal. He is most anxious to oblige and is very fussy.

THE POSTMASTER is so simple that he can only be called naive.

The other parts call for no special comment. Their originals are in any case always with us.

The cast should be specially attentive to the concluding tableau. The final speech, from the Gendarme, must stun everybody on the stage, immediately and simultaneously, like an electric shock. The entire company should shift and freeze its position in a single instant. An exclamation of astonishment must be given by all the female characters simultaneously, as it were from a single pair of lungs. If this business is not properly performed the whole effect may be ruined.

This translation of *The Government Inspector* was first performed by the Royal Shakespeare Company on 19 January 1966, at the Aldwych Theatre, London, with the following cast:

THE MAYOR, Antòn Antònovich Skvoznik Dmukhanovsky (*Civil Mayor Second Class, Anton Ant'n'ich*)	Paul Rogers
THE JUDGE, Amos Fyòdorovich Lyàpkin-Tyàpkin (*Civil Captain First Class, Amos Fy'do'vich Flapkin-Slapkin*)	Brewster Mason
THE CHARITY COMMISSIONER, Artèmy Philìpovich Zemlyanìka (*Civil Captain Third Class, Art'y Ph'lip'ich Zemolina*)	Paul Hardwick
THE SCHOOLS SUPERINTENDENT, Lukà Lukìch Khlòpov (*Civil Officer Second Class, Luna Lunich Plopov*)	David Waller
THE POSTMASTER, Ivàn Kuzmìch Shpyòkin (*Civil Officer Sixth Class, Ivan Goosmich Myopik*)	David Warner
THE DISTRICT PHYSICIAN, Christiàn Ivànovich Hùbner (*Civil Officer Seventh Class*)	Terence Greenidge
THE POLICE INSPECTOR, Lieutenant Stefàn Ilyich Ukhovyòrtov (*Stepan Bullbich*)	Ted Valentine
PETER IVÀNOVICH BÒBCHINSKY, *a landowner*	Tim Wylton
PETER IVÀNOVICH DÒBCHINSKY, *a landowner*	Charles Kay

IVÀN ALEXÀNDROVICH KHLYÈSTAKOV, *a Government clerk from St Petersburg*	Paul Scofield
OSSÌP, *his servant*	Eric Porter
ANNA ANDRÈYEVNA, *the Mayor's wife*	Patience Collier
MARIA ANTÒNOVNA, *the Mayor's daughter*	Patsy Byrne
THE LOCKSMITH'S WIFE	Pamela Buchner
THE SERGEANT'S WIDOW	Estelle Kohler
KORÒBKIN'S WIFE	Madoline Thomas
SCHOOLS SUPERINTENDENT'S WIFE	Frances de la Tour
ABDÙLLIN, *a shopkeeper* (*Abd'in*)	Donald Burton
MÌSHKA, *the Mayor's servant*	John Kane
A WAITER, *at the inn*	Timothy West
A GENDARME, *from St Petersburg*	Stanley Lebor

FYÒDOR ANDRÈYEVICH LYULYUKÒV (*Lulukov*)	⎫	Paul Starr
	⎬ *retired officials*	
IVÀN LÀZAREVICH RASTAKÒVSKY	⎪	Jonathan Hales
STEPÀN IVÀNOVICH KORÒBKIN	⎭	Timothy West

SVISTUNÒV (*Fistov*)	⎫	Jeffery Dench
PÙGOVITZIN (*Pushov*)	⎬ *police constables*	
DYERZHIMÒRDA (*Dustov*)	⎭	John Corvin

Shopkeepers, Guests, Townspeople, Petitioners

Directed by Peter Hall
Designed by John Bury and Elizabeth Duffield

Act One

A room in the MAYOR'S *house. On stage are assembled the*
CHARITY COMMISSIONER, *the* SCHOOLS SUPERINTENDENT,
the JUDGE, *the* DISTRICT PHYSICIAN *and the* MAYOR.

MAYOR. [Well, gentlemen! I've asked you all here today
because] I've got some very nasty news for you. [It looks as
if] there's a Government Inspector on his way to see us.

JUDGE. On his way . . . *here?*

CHARITY COMMISSIONER. A Government Inspector?

MAYOR. A Government Inspector from Petersburg. Under
secret orders. And travelling – incognito!

JUDGE. That's terrible!

CHARITY COMMISSIONER. Dear God, what'll become of us!

SCHOOLS SUPERINTENDENT. And under secret orders [too.]

MAYOR. I knew something horrible was going to happen. I
was warned. I had this dream, last night, about these rats.
Huge black fellers, [they were,] I never seen such rats in my
life. In they come, two of them, very slow . . . creeping
closer and closer all night through. Then they give a
horrifying sniff – and turn tail and walk off. And this
morning, there was this letter from Chmikhov – (*To the*
CHARITY COMMISSIONER.) – you know him, Artemy
Philipovich. Listen to this, now. 'Dear Friend and Benefac-
tor' (*He mumbles, skipping through it.*) '. . . want to . . . tell
you . . . five hundred roubles . . . hasten to . . .' Ah! here we
are, 'and hasten to warn you that a Government official is
on his way to inspect the province, and our district in
particular. I have this from an absolutely reliable source.
This Inspector is travelling incognito . . . (*He looks up.*) – *in-
cog-nito-o* d'you see? – (*He reads.*) – and introduces himself

under a different name in each district. I know that you, like everyone else, have your little weaknesses, you're much too sensible to say no to the perquisites of your office . . .' (*He coughs and looks around.*) Yes, well, we're all friends here . . . '. . . so I advise you to take every precaution you can, as he may turn up at any moment – if, indeed, he isn't already living among you – incognito! My sister Anna Kirilovna and her husband are staying with us. Ivan Kirilovich has put on a lot of weight and never stops playing the fiddle . . .' Yes, well, the rest of it's just family matters, d'you see . . . There you are. Now you know.

JUDGE. [This is incredible! What's it all about?

SCHOOLS SUPERINTENDENT. Yes, Anton Antonovich,] why should they want to inspect *us*?

MAYOR. It's the whim of fate, my friends. So far it's always been other districts, but our luck's changed now!

JUDGE. Anton Antonovich, it's my belief there's more to it than that. It's a political move, that is. It's my belief there's going to be a war, and they're sending an Inspector round to look for traitors!

MAYOR. War? Traitors? What are you talking about? This isn't a frontier town, is it? You could gallop for three years without reaching a foreign country.

JUDGE. You're wrong, Anton Antonovich. The authorities in Petersburg and Moscow are cleverer than you think. They may be a long way away, but they know everything there, let me tell you, *everything*!

They are all terrified.

MAYOR. Well, that's as may be, we shall soon find out; at least you've been warned. I've taken certain percautions myself, you'd best do the same, all of you. 'Specially you, Artemy Philipovich! (*To the* CHARITY COMMISSIONER.) This Inspector, he's sure to visit your hospital, you'd best see it's tidied up a bit. Give those patients of yours some clean night-caps, clean sheets, give them a good wash, last time I saw them they all looked like chimney sweeps!

CHARITY COMMISSIONER. We haven't got any sheets. . . .

MAYOR. Well, buy some, you've been charging for them for

twenty years, haven't you? [And label your patients, put a notice over their beds in some foreign language – Latin, if you can – with a list of dates and diseases, that sort of thing.] And stop them smoking that foul tobacco, a civilised man can't breathe in the place. You'd best throw half of them out anyway, you've got far too many, the Inspector'll think the doctor doesn't know his business.

CHARITY COMMISSIONER. He's a splendid doctor, [we've got everything nicely organised.] Leave it to nature, that's what we say. There's no point in spending a fortune on expensive medicines. Man's a simple creature, if he's going to get well, he'll get well and if he's going to die, then he'll die. Anyway, the doctor's a German, he doesn't understand a word anyone says.

DISTRICT PHYSICIAN (*beaming*). Ja. Onderstand everyt'ing!

MAYOR. Ha! And you, Amos Fyodorovich, you'd best do something about that courthouse of yours, the place is like a farmyard. Tell the porter to move his geese out of the vestibule for a start, the petitioners have to sit there and have their feet pecked at for hours on end. [Of course the porter should be encouraged to keep poultry, but couldn't you persuade him to keep them somewhere else? It's not the thing in a magistrate's court, d'you see. I've been meaning to speak to you about it for a long time.

JUDGE. Don't worry about that, I'll see he kills them today. Perhaps you'd come to dinner tonight, Anton Antonovich?]

MAYOR (*ignoring the invitation*). Your courtroom, Amos Fyodorovich, it's full of rubbish! All your hunting gear lying about, riding crops in the dossier cupboard, boots up on the bench, it's a terrible sight. I know you're fond of hunting, but you clear all that away until this Inspector's been and gone, you can put it all back later. And that clerk of yours! Very clever man, I daresay, but he stinks of vodka day and night! [It's not the thing for an officer of the law. That's another thing I've been wanting to speak to you about, only I keep forgetting. He ought to do something about it, eat garlic or onions or get Doctor Christian to give him some medicine.

DISTRICT PHYSICIAN. Ja, garlick. Gut! (*He beams.*)]

JUDGE. He says it's his natural smell. [He says his nurse dropped him when he was a baby, and he's smelt of vodka ever since.]

MAYOR. Well, [if it can't be helped, it can't.] I just thought I'd mention it, that's all. As for what Chmikhov calls 'our little weaknesses', that's not for me to talk about. No man is without sin, because that's the way the good Lord made us. [Voltaire can say what he likes, but he's a sinner just the same.

JUDGE. Depends what you mean by 'sin', Anton Antonovich.] There are sins and sins. I don't mind admitting I take bribes – but only thoroughbred puppies, you can't call that a sin.

MAYOR. Thoroughbred puppies are still bribes.

JUDGE. But not sinful bribes, Anton, there's the difference. Now if a man accepts a fur coat worth five hundred roubles, or a shawl for his wife . . .

MAYOR (*quickly*). That's no worse than accepting thoroughbred puppies, a bribe's a bribe. What's more, Anton, you don't believe in God. You never go to church! I am firm in my faith, at least. But you, when you go on about the Creation and all that, you make my hair stand on end!

JUDGE. I'm entitled to my opinions. I can think for myself!

MAYOR. That's dangerous, [too much thinking can be worse than none at all. Anyway, I only mentioned your court-house in passing, nobody'd be such a fool as to want to go in there, it ought to have fallen down long ago. It must be under divine protection.] And you, Luka Lukich – your teachers! [You're the Schools Superintendent,] you ought to have done something about them long ago. I know they're clever men, educated and that, but they seem a funny lot to me. There's that one – you know, whatsisname, the one with the twisted nose – can't stand up in front of class without pulling the most terrible faces. [Like this, d'you see. (*He pulls a face.*)] Now that's all right, pulling faces to the boys, that's all part of their education, I suppose, but what happens if he pulls them at the Inspector?

SCHOOLS SUPERINTENDENT. [But what can I do? I've told
him but he takes no notice. The other day, when Prince
Miloffsky called in to look round the school, he was pulling
such scary faces the Prince accused me of letting the boys
be taught by a freethinker!

MAYOR. That's terrible, terrible! And what about that History
master? Very clever, very brainy, knows his subject inside
out, I'm sure, but why does he have to get so excited? He's
all right on the Assyrians and the Babylonians, but I heard
him once on Alexander the Great and I thought the school
was on fire, the way he carried on. He jumped out of his
desk, snatched up his chair and smashed it to the ground. I
know Alexander was a hero, but that's no excuse for
breaking up Government property, is it?]

SCHOOLS SUPERINTENDENT. It's just his enthusiasm. I've
told him about it several times, but he always says, 'I would
lay down my life in the cause of learning.' . . . You can't say
much to that, can you?

MAYOR. That's a funny thing about life – all the cleverest men
are mad. Mad! They either drink themselves to death, or
pull faces that would shame the devil.

SCHOOLS SUPERINTENDENT (*gloomily*). I wouldn't want my
worst enemy to work in education. Everyone's afraid of
everyone else, everyone interferes with you, everyone wants
to prove he's cleverer than you are. It's a dog's life.

MAYOR. It wouldn't matter, all that, if it wasn't for this
damned Inspector, this in-cog-nit-o! Any moment he could
come bursting in through that door (*He points.*), looking for
you. 'Ah, here you all are,' he'll say. 'Where's that Judge? –
Lyapkin-Tyapkin – hand him over. And who's the Charity
Commissioner? – Zemlyanika. Let me have him . . .
District Physician? – Doctor Christian – come with me!' It's
terrifying, terrifying!

THE DISTRICT PHYSICIAN *laughs his head off.*

Enter the POSTMASTER. *They all jump with fear.*

POSTMASTER. What's all this I hear about a Government
Inspector?

MAYOR. When did you hear?

POSTMASTER. Just now. Peter Ivanovich Bobchinsky came into the Post Office to tell me.

MAYOR. What do you make of it, then?

POSTMASTER. It's obvious.

MAYOR. What's obvious?

POSTMASTER. There's going to be a war with the Turks.

JUDGE. Just what I said!

MAYOR. Nonsense!

POSTMASTER. It'll be war with the Turks, you'll see. Those damned French are behind it, as usual, they'll never learn. Well, they'll get more than they bargained for this time!

MAYOR. Stop being an idiot, Ivan Kuzmich! We're the ones who'll get more than we bargained for, not the Turks. (*He hands the* POSTMASTER *his letter.*) Read this!

POSTMASTER. Aha, a letter! That's different. Perhaps it won't be war with the Turks, after all.

MAYOR. *Read!* (*Pause.*) Well?

POSTMASTER. Well, what?

MAYOR. What about it? How do you feel about it?

POSTMASTER. What about you? How do you feel about it?

MAYOR. Me? [Oh, it's nothing to me,] I'm not worried. Well, of course, there's the shopkeepers, a few tradesmen, I know, I know, they're always complaining about me, but as God's my judge, if I ever accepted a penny from anybody it was all done without a scrap of ill-feeling on either side . . . (*He takes the* POSTMASTER*'s arm and leads him downstage.*) D'you think someone could have sent in a – a secret report about me? Whyever else should they send an Inspector down here? Listen, Ivan Kuzmich, don't you think that – for all our sakes – you could just take a peek at all the letters that come through your Post Office? You know, unseal them, quick look, seal them up, no harm done? [Then if there's nothing nasty there, no denunciation or anything, you just send them on.]

POSTMASTER. Actually, I always do, Anton Antonovich. I do it more out of curiosity than as a precaution, though. Some people's letters are so interesting – [you'd be amazed what you can learn,] it's better than the newspapers.

MAYOR. [Anything's better than the newspapers.] But you haven't come across anything about this official from Petersburg?

POSTMASTER. Not from Petersburg, no, but [there's been plenty about officials in Saratov and Kostroma – really juicy stuff, some of it, it's a pity you never saw any of it. And] there was this letter from a lieutenant to his friend, describing some dance he'd been to – very daring, some of it. 'My life is spent in the Elysian fields,' he wrote, yes, yes! 'With orchestras playing, and flags flying, and hordes of beautiful women longing to be my slaves . . .' yes, yes. Oh, there was so much *feeling* in that letter, Anton Antonovich! I had to keep it, I liked it so much. (*He produces the letter.*) Shall I read it to you?

MAYOR. Not now; some other time. But you'll do me that little favour, won't you, Ivan Kuzmich – unseal 'em, quick look, seal 'em up again. Anything compromising, don't hesitate, do your duty, keep it back.

POSTMASTER. Certainly, with pleasure, Anton Antonovich.

JUDGE (*overhearing the last exchange*). You'll find yourselves in trouble, you two, if you're not careful. [One little slip, Ivan Kuzmich, and you'll find yourself reduced to Civil Officer, Seventh Class.] Remember, it only took one spark to set Moscow on fire.

MAYOR. Oh, nonsense! We're not going to make public use of the letters. [It's just a little arrangement between friends.

JUDGE. Mind you, I think you're right, there's trouble in the wind, I can always smell it coming. (*He brings the* MAYOR *downstage.*) By the way, Anton Antonovich, old friend, I've been meaning to give you a little present, only I keep forgetting. A bitch puppy it is, sister to that splendid hound of mine. Of course as far as shooting's concerned, I'm really in clover now. You know Tcheptovich is suing Varhovinsky? Ha! So I get free shooting on both their estates. I could take you along. . . .

MAYOR (*breaking away from him*). Good God, who cares about your free shooting, today of all days.] I can't get this

damned in-cog-nit-o out of my head! I'm sure that any
moment that door's going to open and . . .

The door bursts open and in come BOBCHINSKY *and*
DOBCHINSKY, *out of breath.*

BOBCHINSKY. Something quite extraordinary has happened!

DOBCHINSKY. Something really unexpected!

ALL. What?

What is it?

What's happened?

DOBCHINSKY. You'll never credit it. We went down to the
inn . . .

BOBCHINSKY. Yes, I was going to the inn with Peter
Ivanovich . . .

DOBCHINSKY. Please, Peter Ivanovich, I'm telling it!

BOBCHINSKY. No, no! Please! Let me, let me! You'll never
get it right, let me tell it!

DOBCHINSKY. You'll muddle it all up and forget the best bits,
I know you will!

BOBCHINSKY. I won't, I won't, I'm sure I won't! Don't
interrupt, now, let me tell the story and don't interrupt!
Gentlemen, please, tell Peter Ivanovich not to interrupt!

MAYOR. Heavens above, stop squabbling and speak, for the
love of God! [You've got our hearts in our boots, sit down
and put us out of our misery, one of you!] Here, Peter
Ivanovich, here's a chair for you . . . and one for you, Peter
Ivanovich.

They all seat themselves around the two PETER IVANO-
VICHES.

Now then, what's all this about?

BOBCHINSKY (*to* DOBCHINSKY). Allow me, please! (*He
collects himself.*) W-e-e-e-ll . . . I'll begin at the beginning.
(*To the* MAYOR.) As soon as I had the pleasure of leaving
you, after you'd had that upsetting letter, [I ran off,] do you
see – [Oh, please, Peter Ivanovich, don't interrupt, I know
all of it, all of it! Well, do you see,] I dashed in to see
Korobkin, but Korobkin wasn't at home, so I ran on to
Rastakovsky's but Rastakovsky wasn't at home either, so
then I popped in to see Ivan Kuzmich here – (*He indicates*

the POSTMASTER.) – and he *was* at home, so I gave him the news about this Government Inspector. W-e-e-e-ll, coming away from Ivan Kuzmich I happened to run into Peter Ivanovich . . .

DOBCHINSKY. Near the stall where they sell hot pies.

BOBCHINSKY. Near the stall where they sell hot pies. I met Peter Ivanovich and I said to him: Have you heard the news Anton Antonovich had in his letter? But Peter Ivanovich had already heard all about it from your house-keeper – (*To the* MAYOR.) – Avdotya, who'd been on some errand to Phillip Antonovich Pochechuev, I can't remember what . . .

DOBCHINSKY. To fetch a keg of French brandy.

BOBCHINSKY. To fetch a keg of French brandy. So we went off – Peter Ivanovich and I went off – to see Pochechuev –

DOBCHINSKY. And I said –

BOBCHINSKY. Now, please, Peter Ivanovich, don't interrupt, you mustn't interrupt – we were on our way to see Pochechuev when Peter Ivanovich said to me, 'Let's go into the inn,' he said, 'I've had nothing to eat all day and my stomach's beginning to rumble' – Peter Ivanovich's stomach, that is, do you see – 'let's go into the inn,' he kept saying, 'they've got some fresh salmon in and we could just have a little bite.' S-o-o-o . . . we'd no sooner got into the inn than this young man . . .

DOBCHINSKY. Quite well dressed, but not in uniform . . .

BOBCHINSKY. Quite well dressed, but not in uniform . . . came in and strolled across the room with such a thoughtful expression, do you know, very serious . . . nice manners . . . gestures . . . and a look, do you know, as if he'd got a lot (*He taps his forehead.*) – up *here*! And suddenly I had a kind of presentiment, and I said to Peter Ivanovich here, I said, 'There's more in this than meets the eye,' I said. Yes! Well, Peter Ivanovich called over the innkeeper, you know, Vlass – his wife had a son three weeks ago, such a bright little chap he is, he'll be running an inn like his father one day, you'll see. . . . So Peter Ivanovich asks this Vlass, quietly, do you see, 'Who is that young man?' he asks, and this Vlass says, 'That young man,' he says . . .

DOBCHINSKY. . . . Is an offic –

BOBCHINSKY. Oh, please don't interrupt, Peter Ivanovich, you couldn't possibly tell the story properly, [you've got a lithp,] ever since you lost that tooth you've talked with a whistle. . . . 'That young man,' says Vlass, 'is an *official*, from Petersburg he is, and his name,' says Vlass, 'is Ivan Alexandrovich Khlyestakov, and he's on his way,' says Vlass, 'to Saratov, so he says, and his behaviour,' says Vlass, 'is very peculiar, very peculiar indeed,' says Vlass, 'he's been here nearly two weeks, he's had everything on credit, he hasn't parted with a penny since he arrived and he shows no signs of wanting to leave!' – says Vlass. And it was as he was saying that, that suddenly it dawned on me, and I said to Peter Ivanovich, 'Aha!' I said . . .

DOBCHINSKY. No, Peter Ivanovich, it was me that said 'Aha!' first!

BOBCHINSKY. All right, you said it first, but then I said it. 'Aha' I said . . .

DOBCHINSKY. So did I.

DOBCHINSKY. ⎫
BOBCHINSKY. ⎬ Aha!

BOBCHINSKY (*furious*). . . . we *both* said, 'If he's really going to Saratov,' we said, 'why is he staying here?' we said. '*This*,' we said, 'must be,' we said, 'the *one!*'

MAYOR. The what?

BOBCHINSKY. The official.

MAYOR. What official?

BOBCHINSKY. The official you were warned about in that letter, Anton Antonovich! The Government Inspector!

MAYOR. Dear God, no! Never. It can't be!

DOBCHINSKY. It must be. He doesn't pay his bills, and he doesn't go on with his journey, do you see! Who else could he be?

BOBCHINSKY. It *is* him, it *is*, I swear it! You should have seen how he watched us, how he examined everything! He saw that we were eating salmon – for Peter Ivanovich's stomach, do you see – and he came right across and just stood there, staring down at our plates. It gave me quite a turn.

MAYOR (*closing his eyes*). Lord, have mercy on us sinners! (*To* BOBCHINSKY.) Which room is he in? Did you find out?

DOBCHINSKY. Number five. The one under the stairs.

BOBCHINSKY. Where the officers had that fight last year.

MAYOR. Did you find out how long he's been here?

DOBCHINSKY. A fortnight. He arrived on St Basil's Day.

MAYOR. Mother of God protect us! A fortnight! In the last fortnight the Sergeant's widow's been flogged, the convicts haven't been fed, the streets haven't been swept, the whole town's like a cess-pit! [Oh, the disgrace! The ignominy!] (*He clutches his head.*)

CHARITY COMMISSIONER. Well, Anton Antonovich, what are we going to do? Shall we all go along to the Inn . . . ?

JUDGE. No, no, let the priests and the tradesmen go along first, that's the proper thing. A good reputation stands still, it's the bad ones that run like the wind.

MAYOR. Reputation be damned. Let me handle this my way, please. It's a stupid mouse that only knows one hole. [We've been in some tough spots in the past, and I've always got us out of them – and been praised for it afterwards, too! With God's help we'll get out of this one as well. (*To* BOBCHINSKY.) You say he's a young man?

BOBCHINSKY. Young, yes. Under thirty, I'd swear.

MAYOR. All the better. Young men are easier to deal with, there's always a chink in their armour.] Now, gentlemen, off you go, you've all got muck in your own backyards. I shall take Dobchinsky round to the Inn – just a casual visit, you know, just dropping in to make sure the visitors are being looked after properly, the way I always do. Svistunov!

SVISTUNOV (*rushing forward*). Sir?

MAYOR. Run and fetch the Superintendent, as quick as you can. No, no, don't go, I shall need you here, go and tell someone else to fetch the Superintendent, and then you come back here.

SVISTUNOV *runs off*.

CHARITY COMMISSIONER (*to the* JUDGE). Come on, we best be away, this looks like real trouble.

JUDGE. [I don't know what you've got to worry about, Artemy Philipovich. All you've got to do is hand out a few clean nightgowns and you're in the clear.

CHARITY COMMISSIONER. Clean nightgowns! I'm not worried about nightgowns. There's some stupid regulation says the patients have got to have beef tea every day, but the whole place stinks of cabbage soup, you can't go in there without holding your nose.]

JUDGE. Well, I refuse to get worked up. Who on earth would want to inspect a district courthouse, anyway? [God help anyone who tried to make head or tail of all those books and papers, he'd curse the day he was born.] I've been on the bench here for fifteen years, and I've never yet seen a single report I could understand. Solomon himself couldn't tell right from wrong in this place. . . .

> *The* JUDGE, *the* CHARITY COMMISSIONER, *the* SCHOOLS SUPERINTENDENT *and the* POSTMASTER *go out, colliding in the doorway with* CONSTABLE SVISTUNOV, *who is returning.*

MAYOR (*to* SVISTUNOV). Well, is the carriage ready?

SVISTUNOV. All ready, Your Honour.

MAYOR. Right, go out and . . . no, stop, don't. Wait! Go and fetch me . . . where the devil have all the police got to? Where's Prohorov, he was told to be here.

SVISTUNOV. He's at the station, Your Honour, but he can't go on duty.

MAYOR. Can't? What d'you mean, can't?

SVISTUNOV. He was brought in dead drunk this morning, Your Honour. We put two buckets o' water on'm, Your Honour, but a' won't stand up yet.

MAYOR (*clutching his hair*). Mother of God, what next? Go on out, Constable, quick! . . . no, stop, run to my room first, d'you hear, and fetch me my sword and my new hat. Quick, quick, quick! (*To* DOBCHINSKY.) Come on, Dobchinsky, let's go, then.

BOBCHINSKY. Me too, me too, oh, please, Anton Antonovich, let me come too!

MAYOR. No, no, I'm sorry, Bobchinsky, you can't, you really

can't. [It would be too awkward, d'you see, and] anyway there'd be no room in the carriage.

BOBCHINSKY. I don't mind that, [I'll manage somehow.] I'll run along behind, [I won't try to get in!] I only want to peep through the crack in the door, just to see what happens. . . .

SVISTUNOV enters with the sword and a hatbox.

MAYOR. Here, hold this, Dobchinsky. (*He hands the hatbox to* DOBCHINSKY.) And you hold this, Bobchinsky. (*He hands the hat to* BOBCHINSKY.) (*The* MAYOR *then turns to* SVISTUNOV.) Now run along, fetch the rest of the police, tell them to . . . look at that, I ask you, just look at that blade, all chipped and scratched. Is that a fit sword for a Mayor to carry around? Of course it never occurs to anyone to send me a new one! What a bunch of crooks – I bet they're cooking up a pack of lies about me this very minute! (*Turning to* SVISTUNOV *again.*) [Go and round up the rest of the police, tell them they're each to take a street in their hands . . . what the devil am I saying! – take a broom in their hands and start sweeping the streets – tell them to start near the hotel. And tell them they best sweep it clean – the street, I mean, not the hotel.] And you watch out – yes, you! Oh, I'm on to you, make no mistake! [I know the way my silver spoons have got into the habit of slipping into your bootlegs. You best watch it, my boy!] I'm not as blind as you think I am! What's your game with Schernayev, the draper, eh? Eh? He offers you a couple of yards of broadcloth and what do you do, eh? Walk off with the whole roll, don't you, eh? You best be a bit careful, lad, you're taking more than you're entitled to, you're not a sergeant yet. (*He pushes* SVISTUNOV.) Go on, off with you.

As SVISTUNOV *goes off the* POLICE INSPECTOR *enters.*

Ah, Stefan Ilyich, there you are, where the devil have you been? You want to disgrace me, do you?

POLICE INSPECTOR. I've been out by the gate all the time.

MAYOR. [Nonsense.] Do you realise this Government Inspector is in the town already? What have you done about it, eh?

POLICE INSPECTOR. [What you said. Pugovitzin's taking all my men out to sweep the streets.]

MAYOR. Where's Dyerzhimorda?

POLICE INSPECTOR. Gone to see if the fire-engine's working.

MAYOR. Good. And Prohorov? I'm told he's drunk.

POLICE INSPECTOR. He's out cold. You can't make an empty sack stand up.

MAYOR. [How d'you let that happen, then?

POLICE INSPECTOR. There was a fight on the outskirts yesterday and I sent Prohorov to settle it. He came back absolutely stoned, I don't know why.]

MAYOR. Savages! Now listen to me. Station Pugovitzin on the bridge, he'll look very impressive there, he's tall. Get some of the others to pull down that rotten fence by the cobbler's and stick up a few police notices as if there was some public building going on. No, stop! [Dear God,] I forgot all about the pile of stinking rubbish behind that fence, [forty carts wouldn't shift that lot in a week!] God, what a cess-pit this town is! [Put up a fence, a monument, anything, anywhere, and before you can turn round it's been smothered in rubbish, the devil knows where it all comes from. (*He sighs.*) Now then, another thing, if this damned Inspector comes nosing around any of your men, asking them if they're happy in their work, they're to say, straight out: 'Yes, Your Honour, perfectly happy.' D'you see. And if any of them aren't happy, I'll give them something to be unhappy about, afterwards, just you tell them that, Stefan Ilyich.] Ah me, I'm a sinful man! (*He picks up the hatbox.*) If God sees we get through all this, I'll light Him the biggest candle He's ever seen! I'll make every rotten tradesman in the town give me a hundredweight of wax for that candle, [you wait and see!] (*He prays.*) Dear God, protect us! (*To* DOBCHINSKY.) Come on, Dobchinsky, let's go!

He puts the box on his head.

POLICE INSPECTOR. That's a hatbox, Anton Antonovich, not a hat.

MAYOR (*flinging the box down*). I can see that, you fool! Listen,

[I've thought of something else!] If this Inspector asks about the chapel for the hospital – you know, the one we got a grant for five years past – don't forget, it burnt down. I sent in a report about it. Some idiot's bound to forget and say it was never started, I just know they will. And tell Constable Dyerzhimorda to keep his fists to himself – he seems to think the best way to keep order is to give everyone a black eye, as a matter of principle. (*He starts to go, then runs back.*) And don't let the soldiers out in the street half naked! Every time I go near the barracks, there they are, walking about in nothing but their shirts, it's a scandal – why can't they be issued with trousers?

He rushes out, followed by the others. Enter the MAYOR'S WIFE *and their daughter,* MARIA.

ANNA (*off*). Where are they? Dear God, where's everyone gone? (*Coming through the door.*) Anton! Antosha! Toni! Where are you? (*To* MARIA, *very fast.*) It's all your fault, girl, you and your fussing. 'Wait while I pin this, wait while I tie that . . . !' (*She runs to the window, leans out and calls.*) Toni! Where are you off to? What's happening? Is it the Inspector? Has he got a moustache? What sort of moustache has he got? What?

MAYOR (*off*). Later, my dear, later.

ANNA. Later, what does he mean, later? What's the use of later? (*Shouting.*) Tell me his rank at least, Antosha! Is he a colonel? (*She gives up. To* MARIA.) There, he's gone! I'll make him pay for that! And as for you! (*Mimicking.*) 'Oh, Mamma, Mamma, wait for me, Mamma, help me fasten my collar, Mamma . . .' And now see what happens, we know nothing, nothing! You and your vanity! Just because the Postmaster is here you go prinking and preening over the mirror. You think he's sweet on you, but the moment your back's turned he doesn't even know you exist, so!

MARIA. [Never mind, Mamma, it can't be helped now.] We'll know all about it in an hour or two.

ANNA. Oh, thank you very much, that's lovely! Why stop at an hour, though, why not a month or two while you're at it?

(*She leans out of the window.*) Hey, Avdotya, have you heard anything, eh? Has anyone arrived?

AVDOTYA (*off*). He just waved me aside!

ANNA. Dear God, what a fool that girl is! What d'you mean, waved you aside, you shouldn't have let him wave you aside, you could have jumped in front of him, couldn't you? Idiot, you're as bad as Maria, all you two think of is young men, I know!

AVDOTYA (*off*). They were too quick!

ANNA. What? They were too quick! Well, you be quick too, go on, run after them, find out where they've gone, and find out about this stranger, I want to know everything, everything, d'you hear? Look through the keyhole if you have to, see what colour his eyes are, what sort of moustache he's got, whether he's handsome or not . . . and mind you come straight back! Go on, don't just stand there, hurry, hurry, hurry. . . .

She is still shouting as the curtain falls.

SCENE TWO

A small room at the hotel; bed, table, chair, trunk, empty bottle, top-boots, clothes brush. OSSIP *lounges on the bed with his boots on.*

OSSIP. Gawd, I'm so hungry! I'm so empty I reckon my belly must think my throat's been cut! We don't look no nearer getting home, neither. I dunno. It must be nigh on two months since we left Petersburg. His lordship's been chucking his money about all over the place, and now all we can do is hide away here [with our tails between our legs] and hope for a bloomin' miracle. There'd have been plenty for the whole journey if he didn't have to be so grand every place we stop for the night. (*He mimics* KHLYESTA-KOV.) 'Ai say, Ossip, old chap, cut along and book me the best room in the place, will you? Oh, and order me a decent meal, the very best they've got. Ai simply can't stomach inferior food!' As if he really was somebody! Instead of just a stuck-up little clerk, one cut above an office boy! That's all he is! But he'll put on airs with anybody; out come the cards, and he starts throwing his money away like a millionaire. So now here we are, cleaned out! I'm fed up with him!

Mind you, I'm not saying there's anything against living in the country – not much going on, but then there's less to worry about. [Find yourself a decent wench, you could lie about by the stove all day eating home-made pies, not a care in the world.] But it's not the life for me. Give me Petersburg, every time. You need a bit of the ready, of course, but it's a grand life – theatres, dance-halls, races, the lot! [You can sit next to the officials on the ferry or listen to the officers talking about army life, or what the stars foretell, and all that.] And the way they talk – they call you 'Sir' in the shops, not like here. Very classy in Petersburg. Then there's the women! Take a walk through any of the parks, you can take your pick. Ladies' maids! Parlourmaids! Nursemaids! Housemaids! Aaaaah! (*He smirks and shakes his head.*)

[Oh, it's all polish and politeness in Petersburg! Everyone treats you like a gent! You feel a bit tired and you hop in a cab, lean back, take your ease like a lord! And if you don't happen to feel like paying, you just hop off again – there's a back door to every house, you just nip in one way and out the other, easy. Ah, that's the life!]

Only trouble is, it's all up and down with his lordship. One minute you're stuffing yourself silly, the next you're bloody starving . . . like now. I don't know what to do with him. His old man sends him money enough, but soon as he gets it – whoosh! He's off on the spree again, driving about in cabs all day, showing himself off at the opera every night, and inside a week he's floggin' his clothes again. And he'll let things go for next to nothing – a jacket worth a hundred and fifty – finest English cloth, the latest cut – he'll take a mouldy twenty-five for it. And trousers – he practically gives his trousers away! He'll go on till he hasn't got a shirt to his back; I've seen 'im walking about naked under his overcoat, it's terrible.

If only he'd get down to his job! He never goes near the office! He'd rather swank up and down the Nevsky or lose all his money at cards. If only the old master knew! (*To an imaginary Khlyestakov.*) Civil Servant or no Civil Servant, he'd up with your coat-tails and give you such a hiding you wouldn't sit down for a week. What I say is, if you've got a job to do, do it, and no mucking about.

Gawd, I'm so hungry I could eat a salt mine. And the landlord says no more grub till we've paid for what we've had – that means no more grub. I'd give my eye-teeth for a bowl of cabbage soup . . . aye, aye, somebody coming, sounds like his lordship. . . .

He jumps off the bed.

Enter KHLYESTAKOV.

KHLYESTAKOV. Here, take these. (*He hands* OSSIP *his hat and cane.*) You've been lounging on my bed again.

OSSIP. Lounging on your bed! What you mean? You think I've never seen a bed before?

KHLYESTAKOV. You've been lounging on it, you liar. Look, it's all mussed up!

OSSIP. What would I want with your rotten bed? I've got legs, I can stand, can't I? What do I want a bed for?

KHLYESTAKOV (*pacing up and down*). See if there's any tobacco left in the packet.

OSSIP. Ho, very likely! You know you smoked the last scrap four days ago . . . and that was dust.

KHLYESTAKOV (*pacing, twisting his mouth in different ways, then speaking, loud and determined*). Now, listen to me, Ossip . . .

OSSIP. Well, what?

KHLYESTAKOV (*still loud, but less assured*). You go down . . .

OSSIP. Down? Down where?

KHLYESTAKOV (*almost pleading*). Down to the dining room . . . Tell them . . . ask them . . . to send me up some lunch!

OSSIP. Not likely.

KHLYESTAKOV. What!

OSSIP. I don't feel like it.

KHLYESTAKOV. How dare you!

OSSIP. It's a waste of time, they won't send anything. The landlord said we'll get no more to eat until we pay the bill.

KHLYESTAKOV. What a nerve! The impudence of it!

OSSIP. He says he's going to the Mayor about it. 'You've been here over two weeks,' he says, 'and I haven't seen the colour of your money yet,' he says, 'you're nothing but a couple of common crooks,' he says – straight out.

KHLYESTAKOV. And what a kick you get out of repeating it, don't you?

OSSIP. 'If everyone was like you,' he says, 'the place'd be full of people living at my expense,' he says. 'I'm having no more mucking about,' he says, 'I'm going straight to the Mayor and have you two put in jail.'

KHLYESTAKOV. Shut up, you fool! [That's enough, now!] Get off down those stairs and tell them to send me up some lunch at once. Go on, move!

OSSIP (*gloomily*). I better tell the landlord to come and see you hisself.

KHLYESTAKOV. I don't want the landlord, I want the lunch! Go and tell him that!

OSSIP. But he won't . . .

KHLYESTAKOV (*wildly*). Oh, go on, get out! Bring the landlord if you want to, bring anyone you like, damn you!

He pushes OSSIP *out.*

It's a terrible thing, being as hungry as this. I thought a bit of a walk would help, but it's just made me hungrier than ever. If only I hadn't had such a good time at Penza, we'd still have some money to get home on. It was that infantry captain who finished me off. Had this amazing gift for dealing himself the ace! He can't have sat down with us for more than fifteen minutes, but he picked me clean as a bone! Wonderful! I'd like to have another go at that fellow sometime. There won't be anyone like him in this filthy little dump, that's certain. . . . They won't even give you a cabbage on tick, I've never met such a miserly bunch!

He walks up and down whistling. Enter OSSIP *and the* WAITER.

WAITER. The landlord sent me to see what you want, sir.

KHLYESTAKOV. Ah! Good! Well, my dear chap, how are you, eh?

WAITER. Thank you, sir, I'm very well, sir, thanks be to God.

KHLYESTAKOV. Good, good! And how's business, eh? Everything flourishing?

WAITER. Oh, yes, sir, very busy, thanks be to God.

KHLYESTAKOV. Busy, eh? Plenty of visitors?

WAITER. Plenty enough, sir, thank you . . . and . . . er . . .

KHLYESTAKOV. And thank God, eh? Good, good. Well, now, old chap, they seem to have forgotten about my lunch down in the kitchen, and I've got an appointment this afternoon, so if you'd just nip down and hurry them up a bit. . . .

WAITER. I'm sorry, sir, but the landlord says as we're not to serve you no more. He says as he's going to complain to the Mayor about you, sir.

KHLYESTAKOV. Complain! What's he got to complain about? I'm the one to complain, not him! I've got to eat, haven't I? Everyone's got to eat! I shall waste away to nothing if I don't eat.

WAITER. I know, sir. Only the landlord says, 'I'm not giving him another crust till he's paid for what he's already 'ad.' His very own words, sir.

KHLYESTAKOV. But can't you tell him . . . explain to him . . . I mean, make him see reason . . . ?

WAITER. What can I say, sir?

KHLYESTAKOV. Tell him I've got to eat, of course! It's serious, he can't just let me starve! Money – what's money? You can't eat money, he'll get his money tomorrow, next week, sometime. It's all right for him, he's just a filthy peasant, he's probably used to going without, but he can't let a civilised man like me go hungry, it's ridiculous!

WAITER. I'll tell him what you say, sir.

The WAITER *and* OSSIP *go out.*

KHLYESTAKOV (*pacing*). What am I going to do if he still refuses? I've never been so hungry in my life! I suppose I could sell some clothes . . . my trousers . . . ? No, no, I mustn't, it's better to starve, I simply must arrive home in my Petersburg suit. It's a pity Ossip stopped me hiring that carriage, it would have been great turning up at home in my own carriage, dashing over to see a neighbour with all the lamps shining and Ossip perched up behind in some sort of livery, just like a real footman. (*Drawing himself up, playing the footman.*) 'Ivan Alexandrovich Khlyestakov, from Petersburg, is making his calls. Is the family in residence, my good fellow?' Bah! They wouldn't even know what 'in residence' means, the peasants. They're so crude they just push straight into a drawing room like a pack of bears. But I, I would drift elegantly over to the prettiest daughter . . . (*In foul French.*) 'Mademoiselle, enchanté . . .' (*He bows and scrapes.*) 'Mais vous sommes si beaux . . .' (*He grimaces.*) God, I'm so hungry I feel sick!

He holds his stomach.

Enter OSSIP.

Well?

OSSIP. They're sending up some lunch.

KHLYESTAKOV (*clapping and bouncing*). Dear God, how marvellous, lunch, lunch!

WAITER (*entering with a loaded tray*). Landlord says that's the very last time, now.

KHLYESTAKOV. 'Landlord says!!' Who cares about the rotten landlord! What have you brought?

WAITER. There's some soup, and a roast.

KHLYESTAKOV. What? Only two courses?

WAITER. That's all there is, sir.

KHLYESTAKOV. That's absurd, I'm not putting up with that! Go and tell him it's not enough.

WAITER. Landlord says it's too much, sir.

KHLYESTAKOV. And where's the gravy?

WAITER. There isn't any gravy, sir.

KHLYESTAKOV. Well, why not, eh? Tell me why not? I saw gravy with my own eyes this morning when I was passing

the kitchen. And a lot of other things. There were two
horrid little men in the dining room stuffing themselves
with fresh salmon. Isn't there any of that left?

WAITER. Well, there is, sir, and then again, there isn't.

KHLYESTAKOV. What do you mean, 'Is, isn't'?

WAITER. In a manner of speaking, sir.

KHLYESTAKOV. No salmon?

WAITER. Only for the best customers, sir.

KHLYESTAKOV. Oh, you fool!

WAITER. Yes, sir.

KHLYESTAKOV. You're no better than a pig!

WAITER. No sir.

KHLYESTAKOV. Why should there be salmon for them and
not for me, eh? Why? What's the difference between one
traveller and another, eh?

WAITER. There is a difference, sir.

KHLYESTAKOV. Well? What is it?

WAITER. Some of them pays their bills, sir.

KHLYESTAKOV. Nonsense! I can't argue with an idiot! (*He
ladles out some soup and eats greedily.*) What's this? You call
this soup? They've just poured hot water into a dirty pot!
It's got no taste at all! It just stinks of greasy dishes! I can't
eat this, go and get something different.

WAITER. I'll take it away then, sir. Landlord said if you didn't
like it you needn't have it.

KHLYESTAKOV (*protecting the food with his arms*). Leave it,
leave it, you fool! You may be in the habit of treating your
guests like this, but let me tell you I'm not in the habit of
putting up with it! (*He drinks some soup.*) My God, what a
foul brew! (*He goes on drinking.*) I can't believe anyone alive
has ever tasted worse! Look, there's feathers floating in it!
Whoever heard of feather soup? Here, Ossip, there's a bit of
soup left if you want it. (*He tackles the roast.*) Good God,
what on earth's this? It can't be meat!

WAITER. What is it, then?

KHLYESTAKOV. God alone knows, but it isn't meat, it's
absolutely solid! They must have cooked the chopper by
mistake. (*He tears at the meat.*) Oh, the crooks! Fancy giving

people rubbish like this, it's enough to give you lockjaw. (*He is chewing madly.*) It's criminal! Look, it's like the bark of a tree! Ugh! (*He picks his teeth.*) Like splinters, won't come out! Filthy stuff, it'll probably turn my teeth black as coal! (*He wipes his mouth.*) Well, what else is there?

WAITER. Nothing, sir.

KHLYESTAKOV. Nothing! Oh, the brigands! No, gravy, no pudding, what do these scum think they're up to? They make me pay through the nose for a scrap of roast wood and some hot dishwater! It's disgusting. I shall complain to the Mayor!

OSSIP *and the* WAITER *have hurriedly cleared the plates and left.*

It's just as if I'd eaten nothing at all! I've just whetted my appetite. If I had a penny to my name I'd send Ossip out for a bun.

Enter OSSIP.

OSSIP. Here – the Mayor's downstairs . . . asking all sorts of questions about you.

KHLYESTAKOV (*terrified*). What? No! That damned landlord's complained already! Suppose he's come to take me to prison . . . ? Well, what of it, they'd have to treat me like a gentleman, and at least there'd be food. . . . No! No! I won't go, someone might see me, one of those officers or that pretty little daughter of the seed-merchant I've been flirting with, I can't let them all see me being dragged off to prison. Who the devil does he think he is, anyway, this landlord? I'm not some miserable shopkeeper or smelly labourer! (*Screwing up his courage.*) I'll tell him to his face. 'How dare you!' I'll say. 'Who do you think you are?' I'll say. 'Who the hell are you . . . ?'

The doorhandle turns, and KHLYESTAKOV *grows pale and shrinks into himself. Enter the* MAYOR, *shutting the door on* DOBCHINSKY.

KHLYESTAKOV *and the* MAYOR, *both equally terrified, stare at each other in silence for some moments. The* MAYOR *recovers first and comes to attention.*

MAYOR. May I take the liberty of wishing you good-day, sir?

KHLYESTAKOV (*bowing*). Much obleeged, I'm sure.

MAYOR. I hope you'll pardon the intrusion. . . .

KHLYESTAKOV. Not at all.

MAYOR. It's my duty, as senior official in the town, to see that all visitors and persons of rank and quality suffer no inconvenience. . . .

KHLYESTAKOV (*breaks in, stammering, but raising his voice as he goes on*). B-b-b-b-but what could I d-d-d-do . . . I'm g-g-going to p-p-pay, I really am, they're sending money from home . . .

Enter DOBCHINSKY, *shutting the door on* BOBCHINSKY.

It's his fault, not mine. The food's uneatable, terrible, the meat's like shoe leather and the soup, God only knows what he puts in the soup. I had to throw some out the window just now. That man's starving me! And the tea . . . you'd never know it was tea, it stinks like fish-glue! Why should I . . . why . . . I don't see why . . .

MAYOR (*intimidated*). Please forgive me, it's really not my fault. The meat in the market's always good, I see to that, it's all brought in by good honest dealers, we've never had a complaint like this before. I really can't imagine where he could get bad meat. But sir, if you aren't satisfied with things here, I'd best escort you to other quarters. . . .

KHLYESTAKOV. No, no, no! I know what you mean with your 'other quarters' – you mean the jail. Well, I won't go! You've got no right, how dare you! I-I-I'm a Government official from Petersburg, I-I-I –

MAYOR (*aside*). Dear God, he's furious! Those damned shopkeepers have told him everything.

KHLYESTAKOV (*wildly bluffing*). You can bring a whole regiment with you, I still won't go! I'll write straight to the Minister, I will! (*He thumps the table.*) Who do you think you are? You . . . you . . . !

MAYOR (*trembling, stands to attention*). Oh, please, sir, have pity on us, don't ruin us! My wife . . . my little children . . . it'll ruin us!

KHLYESTAKOV. What's that got to do with it? Just because you've got a wife and children, you want me to go to jail?

BOBCHINSKY *peeps round the door, and withdraws in alarm.*

Well, I won't, so there!

MAYOR (*trembling*). It was my inexperience, sir, that's all. God knows it was all because of my inexperience, and because I'm paid so little, my official salary couldn't keep us in tea and sugar, I swear to God it couldn't. And if I've ever taken a bribe it's been nothing, nothing – something for the table, a little bit of cloth for a coat . . . trifles. And that story about me having the Sergeant's widow flogged, it's all lies, it's slander, sir, put about by my enemies! There's people here so jealous of my position they'd kill me if they dared!

KHLYESTAKOV. Well, it's nothing to do with me, all that. (*Thoughtfully.*) Why tell me all this – what do I care about your enemies, and some rotten Sergeant's rotten widow? You needn't think you can flog me, the way you did that poor woman. Oh, no, you've got a long way to go before you can do that, the idea of it! I'll pay my bill . . . I'll pay . . . I just don't happen to have any money at the moment, that's all . . . That's why I'm stuck in this ghastly place, I just haven't a penny to pay with.

MAYOR (*aside*). Ar, 'at's a crafty little fellow. That's a broad enough hint, but there's such a fog of words around it you can't be certain. Ah, well – what has to be, has to be. (*To* KHLYESTAKOV.) Sir, if you should happen to be temporarily short of – er – ready money, sir, or of anything else, sir, why, sir, it's my duty to help out visitors, so I'm at your service.

KHLYESTAKOV. Ready money . . . ! Yes, yes, could you, would you, lend me a little, just to pay off that damned landlord . . . a couple of hundred would do . . . possibly even . . . less . . . ?

MAYOR (*handing him a sheaf of notes*). Two hundred, of course. It's a pleasure, please don't bother to count them, it's exactly right.

KHLYESTAKOV (*taking the money*). Much obleeged, I'm sure. Of course, I'll send it straight back the moment I get to my

estate, I never delay over things like that. I can see you're a
real gentleman, sir, and I'm sorry if I misjudged you.
Things will be quite different now. (*He calls.*) Hey, Ossip!

MAYOR (*aside*). He took it like a lamb, thank God. [Things
ought to go a bit easier now.] I managed to slip him four
hundred instead of two.

Enter OSSIP.

KHLYESTAKOV. Ossip, fetch that waiter back here. (OSSIP
goes off.) (*To the* MAYOR *and* DOBCHINSKY.) But why are
you both standing, gentlemen? Please sit down. (*To*
DOBCHINSKY.) Sit down, sir, please.

MAYOR. It's all right, we don't mind standing.

KHLYESTAKOV. No, please, I won't have it, sit down, do! I see
now what kind and generous people you are. I confess that
at first I thought you'd come to . . . (*To* DOBCHINSKY.) Sit
down!

They sit, uneasily. BOBCHINSKY *peeps through the door.*

MAYOR (*aside*). He wants to stay incognito, we'll have to go
along with it. (*Aloud to* KHLYESTAKOV.) We just popped in
– that is, Peter Ivanovich Dobchinsky here, [he's a local
landowner,] and me – thought we'd pop in here and see
how they're treating the visitors. . . . That's part of my
duties, you know, I'm not the sort of Mayor who leaves
everything to look after itself. I take my responsibilities as
an official and a Christian seriously. My only reward is the
occasional pleasure of meeting someone really distinguished, like yourself.

KHLYESTAKOV. The pleasure's mine, sir. If it hadn't been for
you I might have been stuck in this dump for ages – I hadn't
the faintest idea how I was going to pay the bill.

MAYOR (*aside*). Oh, yes, very likely! Couldn't pay his bill,
indeed! (*Aloud to* KHLYESTAKOV.) And may I take the
liberty, sir, of asking you where you might be travelling to?

KHLYESTAKOV. I'm off home, old chap. To my estate in
Saratov.

MAYOR (*aside*). Saratov, he says – and without a blush, too!
I'm going to have to watch this one. (*Aloud.*) Very nice too,
a delightful journey. They say travel broadens the mind,

though on some of these roads it isn't only the mind that gets broadened. . . . I take it you're travelling for pleasure, sir?

KHLYESTAKOV. No. My father sent for me. The old boy's worked up because I haven't been promoted yet, he seems to think they start pinning decorations on you the moment you arrive in Petersburg! I'd like to see how he'd get on if he had to hang around my rotten office all day!

MAYOR (*aside*). Dragging in his old father now, that's a good one! (*Aloud.*) Will you be staying long on your estate, sir?

KHLYESTAKOV. I really can't say. My father's as stupid as a mule, and just as obstinate. He can say what he likes, I just *can't* live anywhere but Petersburg, and there's an end to it. 'I'm not going to waste my life among peasants,' I shall say, 'my soul is a-thirst for culture. The world has changed,' I shall tell him, 'since you were young!'

MAYOR (*aside*). At's a first class liar, no mistake – never dries up, never puts a foot wrong. [Looks as if you could knock him down with a feather, too.] I'll catch him out yet, though. (*Aloud.*) Of course, sir, you're absolutely right. What can anyone do out in the wilds, away from the people who matter. Take my case, now – I can be up all night, slaving away, trying to do my best for the country – but where's the recognition, eh? Who's to know about it? (*He looks round the room.*) This room looks damp to me.

KHLYESTAKOV. Damp? The place is a sewer! And you should see the bed-bugs – they bite like wolf-hounds.

MAYOR. Dear God, that's terrible! A distinguished visitor being exposed to that sort of thing, it's scandalous. Very likely the room's a bit dark for you, too, sir?

KHLYESTAKOV. Like the depths of hell. That damned landlord won't even give me a candle to read by. Now and then one feels like a bit of culture – read an essay or two, scribble the odd poem, but one can't, it's too dark.

MAYOR. I wonder if I might . . . ? Oh, no, I can't. I'm unworthy!

KHLYESTAKOV. What? What is it?

MAYOR. No, really, I'm not worthy.

KHLYESTAKOV. Worthy of what, for heaven's sake?

MAYOR. [If only I dared,] I'd . . . I have this lovely room in my house, d'you see, quite empty . . . full of light . . . quite . . . if only I dared . . . but no, I can't. It would be too great an honour. Please pardon any presumption, it's only my simple nature that makes me want to offer . . .

KHLYESTAKOV. On the contrary, old chap, I'd be delighted, really! I'd much rather be in a private house than in this disgusting tavern.

MAYOR. And I shall be delighted! My wife will be delighted! My daughter will be delighted! I've always put hospitality first, ever since I was a child! Especially when my guest is a real personage like yourself. Oh, please, please don't think I'm flattering you, that's not my way at all. I speak straight from the heart.

KHLYESTAKOV. I'm much obleeged, old chap. I'm the same myself – I just can't stand hypocrites. I like your frankness and cordiality, they're the first things I look for in people. I confess I ask for nothing more in life than honesty and sympathy. Honesty and sympathy, that's all I ask.

Enter the WAITER *and* OSSIP; BOBCHINSKY *peeps round the door again.*

WAITER. You sent for me, sir.

KHLYESTAKOV. Yes, I want the bill.

WAITER. I gave it to you this morning, sir. Again.

KHLYESTAKOV. I don't keep your filthy bits of paper. How much was it?

WAITER. Well, now, you had full dinner the first night, smoked salmon for lunch next day – them you paid for. After that it was all on tick, so . . .

KHLYESTAKOV. Idiot! I don't want a list of what I had, I want to know how much I owe.

MAYOR. Please, sir, don't upset yourself, let it wait. (*To the* WAITER.) You can go. I'll see the bill's paid.

KHLYESTAKOV (*putting his money away*). Yes, of course, much better.

The WAITER *goes off.* BOBCHINSKY *peeps in.*

MAYOR. Would Your Honour perhaps care to look over some of our public buildings, I wonder?

KHLYESTAKOV. Whatever for?

MAYOR. Why, sir, to see how we do things here, how the town's administered, and so on and so forth.

KHLYESTAKOV. Well, all right, if you like.

   BOBCHINSKY *peeps in again.*

MAYOR. You could have a look at the school, see how we teach the children. . . .

KHLYESTAKOV. Oh, certainly, certainly.

MAYOR. And then we could go down to the police station, visit the cells . . . ?

KHLYESTAKOV. Why the police station? . . . I'd much rather see the hospital.

MAYOR. Of course, Your Honour, of course, anything you say! Would you rather go in your carriage or will you do me the honour of sharing mine?

KHLYESTAKOV. I'll come with you, please.

MAYOR (*to* DOBCHINSKY). There won't be room for you.

DOBCHINSKY. It doesn't matter, I'll be all right.

MAYOR (*aside to* DOBCHINSKY). Listen, you've got to run like the wind, deliver a message to my wife. (*To* KHLYESTAKOV.) Will you excuse me, sir, if I just scribble a short note to my wife? She'll want to prepare for such a distinguished guest.

KHLYESTAKOV. Will she really? Well, there's ink here, but I don't think there's any paper. Here, what about this bill, will that do?

MAYOR. Splendid, splendid, thank you. (*He writes, muttering to himself.*) We'll see how things are after he's had a good lunch and a few bottles of wine – get out that local Madeira. It looks innocent enough but a couple of good glasses'd make an elephant stagger. If only I knew a bit more about him, I'd know what to watch out for. There, now hurry!

   He hands the note to DOBCHINSKY, *who moves towards the door. At this moment the door comes off its hinges and* BOBCHINSKY *comes flying into the room on top of it. General exclamations of alarm.* BOBCHINSKY *scrambles up.*

KHLYESTAKOV. I say, have you hurt yourself?

BOBCHINSKY. Do, do, it's dothing, dothing at all, please don't bodder! I've just bruised the bridge of by dose, dat's all. I'll rud over to Doctor Christian's, he's got a barvellous plaster thing, he'll put it right id do tibe.

MAYOR (*furious with* BOBCHINSKY). It doesn't matter, it's nothing. Will it please Your Honour to come now? Your man can bring over your luggage. (*To* OSSIP.) Bring everything round to the Mayor's house, anyone will show you the way. (*He shows out* KHLYESTAKOV *formally*.) No, sir, after you, please! (*He follows, but turns back at the doorway.*) That's typical, typical! Couldn't you find someone else's door to knock down? [Coming tumbling into the room like a circus clown!] (*He takes a few more steps and turns.*) Bah! [Numbskull!]

> The MAYOR *stalks out.* BOBCHINSKY, *head hanging, slowly follows.*

CURTAIN

SCENE THREE

The MAYOR'S *house.*
The MAYOR'S *wife,* ANNA, *and his daughter,* MARIA, *are still standing by the window.*

ANNA. Oh, it's monstrous! Here we are, still hanging about with no idea what's going on, all because of your prinking and preening over the dressing table! I wish I'd never listened to you. Oh, isn't it infuriating! Not a soul in sight, it's just as if the whole town was dead! You'd think they were doing it on purpose!

MARIA. Really, Mamma, [we're sure to know all about it in a few minutes,] Avdotya can't possibly be much longer . . . (*Peering out of the window, she suddenly screams.*) Mamma, Mamma, look, someone's coming, look, right at the end of the street!

ANNA. Where? I can't see anyone. You're always imagining things, girl!

MARIA. There!

ANNA. Oh, yes, so there is! Who is it? It's a man . . . very small . . . dressed like a gentleman . . . oh, who can it be, how maddening, who on earth can it be?

MARIA. It's Dobchinsky, Mamma.

ANNA. Dobchinsky! Don't be ridiculous, you're imagining things again, it's no more Dobchinsky than . . . (*She leans out of the window, waving her handkerchief.*) Hey! You! Come here! Hurry!

MARIA. It really is Dobchinsky, Mamma.

ANNA. Don't contradict me, I tell you it's not.

MARIA. [There, now, look! Wasn't I right?] It's Dobchinsky.

ANNA. Of course it's Dobchinsky, I can see that for myself, what are you arguing about? (*She shouts.*) Come on, hurry, hurry! Oh, why do you walk so slowly! Where is everyone? What? No, tell me from there. What? [Very stern, did you say?] What about my husband? [My husband!] Where's Anton? Oh! (*She moves away from the window in a fury.*) The man's an imbecile, he won't say a word until he gets inside! (*She paces.*)

Enter DOBCHINSKY, *out of breath.*

Well? Aren't you ashamed of yourself? I was relying on you, Peter Ivanovich, I thought I could trust you, but no, you had to go dashing off after them and I'm left here all on my own without getting a word out of anyone! Aren't you ashamed? You asked me to be godmother to your children and then you go and treat me like that?

DOBCHINSKY. As God's my judge, I've run myself to a standstill to get here as soon as this! How d'ye do, Maria Antonovna?

MARIA. How do you do, Peter Ivanovich.

ANNA. All right, all right! Tell me what happened. How did things go?

DOBCHINSKY. Anton Antonovich has sent you a note.

ANNA. But what is he? The visitor? Is he a General?

DOBCHINSKY. No, he's not. But he's as good as a General

every bit as good. Better, in fact. He's so cultured! So . . . impressive!

ANNA. It must be the Inspector that Chmikhov wrote to us about.

DOBCHINSKY. Oh, no doubt about it! And it was me that discovered him – me and Peter Ivanovich!

ANNA. But tell us what's *happened*! Quickly!

DOBCHINSKY. Well, at the moment everything seems to be going smoothly, God be praised. Oh, but he gave poor Anton Antonovich such a stiff reception to begin with! Quite furious, he was, complaining about his room and the food but refusing to come here, and saying he wasn't going to the prison on any account. But then when he realised that the bad food, and that, wasn't Anton Antonovich's fault, and we'd had a bit of a talk, he suddenly calmed down and everything started going much better, thanks be to God. They've gone off now to look at the hospital. You know, for a while Anton Antonovich really did think there'd been a secret report sent in about him! I was even quite scared myself!

ANNA. You've nothing to be scared about – you're not even an official.

DOBCHINSKY. I know, but you can't help shaking a bit when someone really superior is speaking.

ANNA. None of that's important. The thing is, what's he like? Is he old or young?

DOBCHINSKY. Quite young, to look at – but he talks like an old man! 'I'm much obleeged to you, sir . . .' that's the way he talks . . . 'I'd be delighted to accompany you . . .' (*He waves his hand vaguely.*) Oh, all terribly high class! 'I'd like to read and write,' he said to me, 'only this room's so frightfully dark!'

ANNA. But what's he *like*? To look at, I mean? Is he dark or fair?

DOBCHINSKY. More sort of yellow . . . or corn-coloured. And his eyes are quick like a ferret's – they make you feel very uneasy.

ANNA. Let's see what Anton says. (*She reads.*) 'I scribble this

in haste, my dear, just to tell you that my position at first
seemed fraught with danger one half portion of caviar but
putting my trust in the mercy of God two portions pickled
cucumber one-twenty-five . . .' (*She stops.*) I can't understand a word of this, what have pickled cucumbers got to
do with it?

DOBCHINSKY. Anton Antonovich scribbled it on the first
piece of paper he could find – it's a hotel bill.

ANNA. Oh, yes, it's a bill. (*She goes on reading.*) '. . . hum –
hum – the mercy of God, I believe we shall come through
safely in the end. You must hurry and get the spare room
ready for our distinguished guest. The one with the yellow
wallpaper. Don't bother about lunch, we shall have a meal
at the hospital, but make sure there's plenty of good wine.
[Tell Abdullin to send us the best he's got, or I'll turn his
cellar upside down with my own hands!] I kiss your hand,
my dear, and remain, yours, Anton Skvoznik Dmukhanovsky.' Heavens above, we must hurry! Mishka! Mishka!

DOBCHINSKY (*running to the door*). Mishka!

ANNA. How long will they be, Peter Ivanovich?

DOBCHINSKY (*running to the window*). They can't be long
now.

ANNA. What! But you said . . . you ran straight here from the
Inn! And they've gone to the hospital!

DOBCHINSKY. I did, I did, Anna Andreyevna! But I had to
go through the dining room, d'you see, to get out of the
Inn, and there was such a lovely smell of roast ham, I
thought, if I don't snatch a bite now I won't get any lunch
at all today.

ANNA. Peter Ivanovich Dobchinsky!

DOBCHINSKY. Then I ran all the way here, truly I did!

ANNA. It's disgusting! The sheer treachery of it! (*Enter*
MISHKA.) Oh, Mishka, now listen, I want you to run to
Abdullin's . . . no, wait a minute, I'll give you a note, you're
so stupid . . . (*She sits, speaking as she writes.*) I want you to
give this to Sidor, tell him to take it down to Abdullin's and
bring back the wine at once. When you've done that, you
can start cleaning up the spare room, the one with the

yellow wallpaper – put a decent bed in there, make sure there's a wash-stand and everything, d'you understand? Here, take this. Now off you go – and hurry!

DOBCHINSKY. Perhaps I'd better be off, Anna Andreyevna. See how things are going . . . you know . . . at the hospital . . .

ANNA. Go on, then, I'm not keeping you. Traitor!

DOBCHINSKY *slinks out hurriedly*.

Now, Maria, we must think about what we're going to wear. He's from Petersburg, we mustn't give him the chance to laugh up his sleeve at us. You must wear your pale blue with the little flounces, that's the most suitable, and I . . .

MARIA (*wailing*). Oh no, Mamma, not the pale blue, I hate the pale blue! That Lyapkin-Tyapkin girl's always in pale blue, and so is that awful Zemlyanika woman! I shall wear my marigold.

ANNA. Your marigold! Really! When will you learn not to do things just to be contrary? You must wear your blue, because *I'm* going to wear my primrose!

MARIA. Oh, Mamma, please! Primrose doesn't suit you at all. You're not . . .

ANNA. I'm not – what?

MARIA. Not dark enough. You have to have dark eyes to wear primrose.

ANNA. Nonsense, girl! Anyway, I have got dark eyes. They must be dark, otherwise how is it that at cards when I tell my fortune I always get the Queen of Spades?

MARIA. You're much more like the Queen of Hearts, really.

ANNA *starts bundling* MARIA *out*.

ANNA. Rubbish, girl, absolute rubbish!

They go off.

(*Off.*) I don't know what you'll think of next! Me, the Queen of Hearts! How ridiculous! (*Business with a mirror – she speculatively studies herself.*)

The door of the spare room opens and MISHKA *sweeps out some dust.* OSSIP *comes in from the front door carrying a suitcase on his head.*

OSSIP. Where d'you want this?

MISHKA. This way, Dad. In here.

OSSIP. Hold on a tick, let me catch me breath. Whew! Wot a load! Still . . . a sack of fevvers'd feel heavy on an empty belly!

MISHKA. Will that General of yours be here soon?

OSSIP. What General?

MISHKA. Your master, of course.

OSSIP. My master? Did you say 'General'?

MISHKA. Isn't he a General, then?

OSSIP. Oh, yes – he's very general.

MISHKA. Is that so? Is he more important than a General, then, or less?

OSSIP. Oh, more, every time!

MISHKA. Is that right! That's why they're making such a fuss about him, then.

OSSIP. Look here, sonny – I can see you're a bright little lad, so what about rustling me up a bite to eat?

MISHKA. They won't have anything ready for you yet, Dad. You wouldn't want to be eating anything plain – you'll be wanting the same as your master gets.

OSSIP. What would you call something plain?

MISHKA. Well . . . there's some cabbage soup, meat pie, and pudding.

OSSIP. Just bring me your cabbage soup, meat pie and pudding. I don't mind eating plain for once! Come on, let's get this thing stowed away. Where is it – in here?

MISHKA. This way, then . . . we can go out through the back. . . .

They go off through the side door, carrying the case between them.

The main door is flung open by two POLICEMEN, *who flank the entrance. Enter* KHLYESTAKOV, *followed by the* MAYOR, *the* CHARITY COMMISSIONER, *the* JUDGE, *the* SCHOOLS SUPERINTENDENT, *the* POSTMASTER, *the* POLICE INSPECTOR, DOBCHINSKY *and* BOBCHINSKY – *the latter with a strip of plaster across his nose. The* MAYOR *gestures grandly at a scrap of paper on the floor; both* POLICEMEN *dive for it, and collide in mid-air.*

KHLYESTAKOV (*expansively*). Well, that's a splendid hospital, splendid. I must say I like the way you show your visitors around the town, it really is most civil! No one ever showed me a thing in any of the other dumps I've been in.

MAYOR. I'm afraid that in some towns the officials are too busy looking after their own interests to do their jobs properly. Here, if I may say so, we think only of how we can earn the approval of our superiors by our vigilance, diligence and the proper administration of Government regulations. So help me, God. Mishka!

KHLYESTAKOV. That was a fine lunch we had – I'm sure I ate too much. Do you eat like that here every day?

Enter MISHKA *with a tray of drinks.*

MAYOR. It was specially prepared, Your Honour, for our very welcome guest.

KHLYESTAKOV. I must say I love good food. That's what life is for – to gather the blossoms of pleasure in full bloom! What was that marvellous fish we had?

CHARITY COMMISSIONER (*bobbing up beside* KHLYESTAKOV). That was salted cod, Your Honour.

KHLYESTAKOV. Really? I'd never have believed it! Cod, eh? Delicious. Where was it we lunched – the hospital, was it?

CHARITY COMMISSIONER. That's right, Your Honour.

KHLYESTAKOV. Yes, I remember now, there were some beds standing around, weren't there? Have all your patients recovered, then? There didn't seem to be any about?

CHARITY COMMISSIONER. [Ah, there's no more'n a dozen or so left now, Your Honour, all the rest've recovered completely.] It's all a question of good management. Ever since I took over that hospital – you may not believe this, sir, but it's true – the patients have been recovering like flies. A sick man can hardly set foot in the place before he's out again, completely cured! [It's not so much your medicines and your treatments, more a matter of really honest and efficient administration.]

MAYOR. Ah, yes, but think what a headache it must be when a man's got a whole town to administer! Think of the hundreds of problems a Mayor has to take on his shoulders

– sanitation, maintenance, public order – the ablest of men might find it too much for him, but here, praise be to God, everything's under good control. There's many a Mayor, do you know, would be feathering his own nest – oh, yes! But when I lie in my bed at night, I have only one thought: 'Almighty God,' I think to myself, 'help me to give absolute satisfaction to my superiors!' [I think of nothing else.] Whether they choose to reward me or not, of course, that's their affair. [If I can see a clean, well-cared-for town, the convicts properly looked after, not too many drunks in the street – there's the satisfaction of a job well done. What more could I want?] I'm not after honours and decorations . . . ! Of course, that sort of thing has its attractions, but as the poet says, compared to the joys of a job well done, everything else is as dust and ashes!

CHARITY COMMISSIONER (*aside*). Listen to him laying it on!

KHLYESTAKOV. Oh, that's all very true! I am myself, I confess, quite fond of philosophising about this and that – sometimes in prose, and sometimes, d'you know, in verse . . . according to my inspiration.

BOBCHINSKY (*to* DOBCHINSKY). Isn't that nicely put, Peter Ivanovich? The way he speaks, it's so . . . you know, you can tell he's studied a lot, can't you?

KHLYESTAKOV. But tell me, aren't there any entertainments in this town . . . you know, places people can drop into for a hand of cards if they feel like it, that sort of thing?

MAYOR (*aside*). Ah-a! I know what he's driving at! (*Aloud.*) God forbid, sir, that anything like *that* should happen in *my* town! I've never held a playing card in my hand in my life, I wouldn't know what to do with it if I did! [I can't bear the sight of a pack of cards, Your Honour.] Why, if I so much as catch sight of a King of Diamonds, it turns my stomach. [I remember once I thought I'd amuse the children by building a house of cards, and so you know, I dreamed of the damned things all night?] I can't think how people can waste their time on such things!

SCHOOLS SUPERINTENDENT (*aside*). And he took a hundred roubles off me only last night!

MAYOR. I prefer to spend my time serving the State.

KHLYESTAKOV. I think that's going a bit far. It all depends how you look at it. Now, of course, if you make the mistake of backing out just when you ought to be doubling your stakes, then. . . . No, no, I can't agree, it's really very jolly to have a hand of cards now and then. . . .

Enter ANNA *and* MARIA, *resplendent.*

MAYOR. Your Honour, allow me to introduce . . . my wife, and my little daughter.

KHLYESTAKOV (*bowing deeply*). Madam, it is indeed a pleasure, if I may say so, to have the pleasure, as it were, of – er – meeting you!

ANNA (*low curtsey*). Our pleasure is much greater, Your Honour, in having so distinguished a guest!

KHLYESTAKOV (*striking an attitude*). No, 'pon my soul, Madam, on the contrary, my pleasure is far, far greater!

ANNA. Oh, sir, now you're just being polite, I'm sure! Won't you please sit down?

KHLYESTAKOV. Madam, simply to stand in such charming company is joy itself! However, if you insist, I'll sit. (*They sit on the sofa together.*) Ah, what happiness it is for me to be sitting with you beside me!

ANNA. I dare not think your words are anything but politeness, sir! Er . . . I imagine, sir, that life in the country must be very distasteful to you after life in Petersburg?

KHLYESTAKOV. Oh, an unimaginable tediosity, Madam! When one is accustomed, comprenny-vous, to life in the best Society, suddenly to find oneself on the road, living in dirty inns amongst uncultured people . . . ! If it weren't for my good fortune today . . . (*He looks up into* ANNA'S *eyes.*) . . . which, I assure you, makes up for everything . . .

ANNA. It must all be so very unpleasant for you, sir.

KHLYESTAKOV. At this moment, Madam, everything is pleasantness itself!

ANNA. Oh, how can you say such things! I'm not worthy of such compliments!

KHLYESTAKOV. On the contrary, Madam, nobody could be more worthy!

ANNA. But I live in the country. . . .

KHLYESTAKOV. And the country itself has its beauties – the woods, the hills, the sparkling streams. . . . One can't, of course, compare it with Petersburg. . . . Ah, Petersburg! Ça, c'est la vivre! You may be thinking that I'm only a clerk, but let me tell you the head of my department is very friendly with me! He'll slap me on the back, so, and say: 'Come round for dinner, old chap' – and just like that! I drop into the office for a few minutes, hand out a few instructions, and leave the old copy-clerk scratching away at his desk. . . . They wanted to promote me, once, but I thought, 'Ah, what's the use?' – and I turned it down. The office porter runs after me with his brush. . . . 'Allow me, Ivan Alexandrovich, allow me! I just want to shine your boots!' (*To the* MAYOR.) Why are you all still standing, gentlemen? Do sit down!

MAYOR.	We can stand . . .
SCHOOLS SUPERINTENDENT.	That's all right, Your Honour . . .
CHARITY COMMISSIONER.	We know our rank . . .

KHLYESTAKOV. Never mind your rank! Sit down!! (*They all scurry to take a seat.*) I won't have any standing on ceremony! I do everything I can, you know, to escape attention, but I'm afraid it's impossible. Wherever I turn up the word seems to get around at once. 'There goes Ivan Alexandrovich Khlyestakov!' they say. Once I was actually mistaken for the Commander-in-Chief – yes! The soldiers all came dashing out of the guardroom to present arms! And later their officer – who's actually a close friend of mine – said 'D'you know, old chap, everyone was convinced you were the Commander-in-Chief!'

ANNA. Well! Would you believe it!

KHLYESTAKOV. It's quite true. Oh, and I know all the pretty actresses in town, of course. Well, you see, I've done quite a lot of writing for the stage . . . amusing little things . . . I go about a lot in the literary world . . . Pushkin's a close pal of mine. Whenever I see him I say, 'Well, Pushkin, old boy, how're things going with you?' And, do you know, he always says exactly the same thing: 'So-so, old chap,' he says, '. . . only so-so.' Ah, he's a great character, is Pushkin!

ANNA. Are you really a writer, then? Oh, how wonderful it must be to be a writer! Do you ever write for the magazines?

KHLYESTAKOV. Oh, yes, I publish in magazines, too. But then I do so many things: novels, plays . . . *Don Juan, Romeo and Juliet, The Marriage of Figaro* . . . I really can't remember all the titles. It was sheer chance that they came to be written anyway. Theatre managers were always pestering me – 'Please, old chap, do write something for us, you know you can!' Eventually, just to get rid of them, I thought 'All right, dammit, I will!' And I sat down, and do you know, I scribbled the whole lot in one evening! They were astonished, I can tell you. (*Pause.*) Yes, well, I've always had a very ready wit. All those pieces in *The Moscow Telegraph* under the name of Baron Brambeus – they're all mine.

ANNA. No! Are you really Baron Brambeus?

KHLYESTAKOV. Oh, yes. Why, there's hardly a writer in the country whose work I haven't rewritten for him at one time or another – I get forty thousand a year doing that sort of thing.

ANNA. I've just been reading a novel called *Youri Miloslavsky* –

KHLYESTAKOV. Oh, yes, that's another of mine.

ANNA. I knew it!

MARIA. But Mamma, it says on the cover that it was written by Zagoskin!

ANNA. You would have to argue, wouldn't you?

KHLYESTAKOV. You're quite right, Madam, there is a book of that name by Zagoskin. But there is also one by me.

ANNA. There! And I'm sure it was yours I read – it's so well written!

KHLYESTAKOV. I must admit, I just live for literature! I keep the best house in Petersburg – everyone knows it, Khlyestakov House they call it. (*To them all with a sweep.*) Gentlemen, if you ever come to Petersburg, you must all come and see me! I give the grandest receptions, you know!

ANNA. I can imagine how magnificent they must be!

KHLYESTAKOV. Oh, they're quite indescribable! In the centre of the table there'll be a huge water-melon costing seven hundred roubles. Then I have soup brought straight from Paris, by steamship, in special containers – you lift the lid, and that Parisienne aroma – ah, there's nothing like it in the world! I go to a dance or a reception every day! Sometimes we make up a four for cards – the English Ambassador, the Foreign Minister, the French Ambassador, the German Ambassador . . . and me. Then, when I get tired of playing cards, I dash up to my little fourth-floor flat and my old cook comes out of the kitchen and I say, 'Take my coat, Mavrushka . . .' Oh, no, what nonsense, I live on the first floor, don't I? And that great staircase of mine, it must be worth . . . ah, you should see my reception hall in the morning, buzzing with counts and princes before I'm even awake . . . bzz, bzz, bzz . . . like a lot of bees, they are. . . . Sometimes you'll even find the Prime Minister there, just hanging about, waiting for me . . .

The MAYOR *and the others rise, awestruck.*

My letters are all addressed to 'Your Excellency', because I was once head of a whole Government department! Oh, yes! Very odd, that was. The director suddenly disappeared, no one knew where, and there were the usual squabbles over who should have the post. There were plenty of generals after the job, and some of them tried to do it, but it was no good, one after another they had to go, it was just too difficult. It looked simple enough at first sight, but when you got down to it, it needed real brains. So in the end they had to send for me. 'Send for Ivan Alexandrovich,' they said – and the messengers went out, all over Petersburg, messenger after messenger, all looking for me! Well, imagine it – thirty-five thousand messengers scurrying about, what about that, eh? 'Ivan Alexandrovich,' they cried when they found me, 'come and take charge of the department!' I was staggered, I wanted to refuse, but then I thought, what if the Tsar heard about my refusal, he'd be offended! So I said to them, 'All right,' I said, 'I'll do it,' I said, 'but I warn you, you'll have to watch out with me, I don't stand any nonsense from anyone . . .' And do you know, when I walked through that department you'd have thought there was an earthquake going on, they were all shaking and shivering so much with fear!

The MAYOR, *etc., shiver.* KHLYESTAKOV *gets more excited.* Oh, I won't be trifled with! I put the fear of God up them! I even had the Privy Council shaking in their shoes! Oh, yes! And why not, eh? That's the sort of man I am, not afraid of anybody. I tell them straight, 'Don't you try to stand in my way, my man!' And they don't! Because I can go anywhere – anywhere! I'm in and out of the Palace at all hours of the day and night – all hours! Why, tomorrow . . . tomorrow . . . they're going to make me . . . a . . . a Field Marshal!

He slips and almost falls, but the officials very respectfully support him.

MAYOR (*tries to speak but is trembling too much*). Your . . . Your . . . Your . . .

KHLYESTAKOV (*very sharp and abrupt*). Well, what is it, what is it?

MAYOR. Yo-Yo – Your –

KHLYESTAKOV (*more sharply still*). I can't understand a word, you're talking nonsense!

MAYOR. Y-your lexency – elxency – Exclensy . . . m-m-might w-w-want to l-l-lie down, have rest . . . your room's ready here, everything you need. . . .

KHLYESTAKOV. Lie down? Rest? Rubbish! Oh, all right, if you like, I suppose I might . . . that lunch was really very good, gentlemen, I'm much obleeged, much ob-leeged! (*He suddenly declaims.*) Salted Cod! Salted Cod! SALTED COD!

He nearly falls, but is helped out by the MAYOR.

BOBCHINSKY (*to* DOBCHINSKY). What a man, Peter Ivanovich! There you have a real man! [Never in my life have I been in the presence of a person of such real importance!] I nearly died of fright, didn't you? What's his rank, d'you think?

DOBCHINSKY. Oh, he must be at least a General!

BOBCHINSKY. He must be the Generalissimo himself! [You heard how he bosses the Privy Council about! I bet any General would have to stand to attention in front of a man like him! Come on,] let's all go and tell Fyodorovich and Korobkin all about it! Goodbye, Anna Andreyevna!

DOBCHINSKY. Goodbye, Anna Andreyevna!

Both run out.

CHARITY COMMISSIONER. I'm terrified! I don't quite know why, but I'm simply terrified. We aren't even in proper uniform – there's no knowing what he may do when he wakes up sober! (*He goes thoughtfully to the* SCHOOLS SUPERINTENDENT.) He'll probably dash off a report to Petersburg! Excuse us, Anna Andreyevna!

They go off.

ANNA. What a fascinating man!

MARIA. He's a darling!

ANNA. He's so refined! You can see at once he's a man of fashion! Those lovely manners ... beautiful gestures! [Gracious me, I do admire young men like that! Such grace and style! And so gallant!] I noticed he couldn't keep his eyes off me!

MARIA. [Oh, Mamma, really!] It was me he was looking at!

ANNA. You? Don't be ridiculous, dear!

MARIA. He was looking at me!

ANNA. [Good God, will the girl never stop contradicting me?] Why should he look at you? Can you tell me one reason on earth why he should look at you?

MARIA. Well, he just did, that's all. When he started talking about his books he stole a glance at me, and I caught his eye. And when he mentioned that game of cards with all those Ambassadors, he was looking straight at me, so there!

ANNA. Well, maybe he did throw you a quick glance, but he was only being polite.

Enter the MAYOR *on tiptoe.*

MAYOR. Sssssh! Sssssh!

ANNA. What's wrong?

MAYOR. I wish I hadn't made him drunk. [I don't know what to think now.] Suppose only half what he said was true? (*He thinks deeply.*) And why shouldn't it be true? When a man's drunk the truth slips out, you can't prevent it. So he plays cards with Ambassadors, he pops in and out of the Palace . . . dear God, [my poor head's going to burst at this rate,] I feel like a man on a scaffold, no mistake.

ANNA. I wasn't a bit frightened of him myself. To me he was just a man of real culture and breeding, that's all. I don't give a fig about his rank.

MAYOR. Aargh! Women! It's nothing but a game to you, is it? You with your silks and satins and feathers and flutters, if you drop a brick all you get is a good hiding from your husband – but your husband gets the sack! Don't you realise you were talking to him the way you talk to any wretched Peter Ivanovich?

ANNA. You worry too much, Antosha. We women know a thing or two, remember. (*She looks meaningfully at* MARIA.)

MAYOR. Ah, what's the use of talking to females!

He opens the door and calls.

Mishka! Mishka! Run and call those two constables, out by the gate, there.

Brief silence.

Ah, it's a funny world. You might have expected to see someone impressive to look at, [but a fancy-looking little whipper-snapper like that!] I dunno! Who'd ever have guessed if we hadn't been warned? [And didn't he just lead us a dance at the Inn this morning! But he's given in now, all right – in fact, he's spilled more of the beans than he need have. That'll be on account of him being so young.] But we know where we are now, all right.

Enter OSSIP.

They all make a dash at him.

ANNA. Ah! Come here now, my good man . . .

MAYOR. Sssh! Ssssh! (*To* OSSIP.) Well? Is he asleep?

OSSIP. Not quite. Just yawning and stretching a bit.

ANNA. Er – hmm – what's your name?

OSSIP. Ossip, Ma'am.

MAYOR. Now that'll do, that'll do! (*To* OSSIP.) Well, old man, have they given you a decent dinner?

OSSIP. Very nice dinner, sir, thank you, sir.

ANNA. Now, tell me . . . I imagine you get quite a few titled people coming to your master's house, eh? Counts and princes, and so on?

OSSIP (*looking round at them with visible cunning*). Oh, yes, Ma'am. All manner of counts and dukes and princes and that.

MARIA. Isn't your master handsome, Ossip! Isn't he?

ANNA. Ossip, tell us what he . . .

MAYOR. That's enough, stop it now! [You're only hindering us with all this stupid questioning! Now, old man, I want you to tell me . . .]

ANNA. What's your master's rank, Ossip?

OSSIP (*cunning again*). Oh, you know – the usual.

MAYOR. God in heaven, how you do keep on!

ANNA (*interrupting*). Ossip, does your master wear uniform at home?

MAYOR. Be quiet, will you? Can't you see this is serious, [it's a matter of life and death.] (*To* OSSIP.) Now I've taken a liking to you, my friend. I know a man likes to have an extra glass of something when he's travelling [– particularly in cold weather –] so here's a couple of roubles I expect you'll find a use for. . . . Go on, hide them away.

OSSIP (*taking the coins*). Very grateful, Your Honour, I'm sure. (*He pulls his forelock.*) May God reward you for helping a poor man, Your Honour.

MAYOR. Not at all, not at all. I'm only too glad to help you. Now then, what sort of things does your master like most when he's travelling, eh?

OSSIP. It all depends, sir, what's available, so to speak. He likes being well-looked-after, and he likes to see I'm well-looked-after too. He's very particular that way. Soon as we've left a place, first thing he asks is, 'Now then, Ossip, did they look after you well back there?' 'No, not very well,' I may say, and that'll be a black mark against them. But of course, Your Honour, I'm a simple man myself, it's nothing to me.

MAYOR. You're a very good man, Ossip, you talk good sense. I gave you something for a little drink, didn't I? Well, here's something for a bite to eat, as well.

OSSIP. Very kind, Your Honour, I'm sure. (*He puts the money away.*) I'll drink to Your Honour's health.

ANNA. Come and talk to me, Ossip. I've got a little something for you, too!

MARIA (*sighing*). Oh, Ossip . . . kiss your master for me! Will you?

KHLYESTAKOV *is heard coughing from the next room.*

MAYOR. Ssssh! (*He walks on tiptoe to listen at* KHLYESTAKOV'S *door. The rest of the scene is played in whispers.*) Not a sound, now, d'you hear! Run along now, you two, you've chattered quite enough.

ANNA. Come on then, Mashenka. There's one fascinating thing *I* noticed about our guest . . . I'll tell you as soon as we're alone.

She sweeps out, MARIA *following.*

MAYOR. Talk, talk, talk – women'll talk your ears right off! (*Turning to* OSSIP.) Now, old chap . . .

Enter, noisily, SVISTUNOV *and* DYERZHIMORDA.

Ssssh! You noisy brutes, clumping in here like a cartload of logs, where the devil have you been, then?

DYERZHIMORDA. Sir, acting on superior orders, we was proceeding . . .

MAYOR. Be quiet! (*He claps his hand over* DYERZHIMORDA'S *mouth.*) You bray like a donkey! [(*Imitating.*) 'We was proceeding' . . . Like a damned brass band!] (*To* OSSIP.) All right, old friend, you can run along now and get anything your master needs. Ask for anything you like, the house is yours.

OSSIP *goes off.*

Now, you two – go and stand by that front door, and don't you move, not one single inch. Don't, [whatever you do,] let anybody in – least of all those damned tradesmen! [You let one of those through and I'll . . . I'll . . . string you up with my own hands!] If you see one of them coming here with anything that looks like a petition, you just pick him up by the scruff and sling him out! Like this, see? (*He kicks out an imaginary petitioner.*) Off you go, then. Shhhh! Sssshhh! *He tiptoes out after the* CONSTABLES.

CURTAIN

Act Two

The same scene, the following morning. Enter, on tiptoe, the JUDGE, *the* CHARITY COMMISSIONER, *the* DISTRICT PHYSICIAN, *the* POSTMASTER, *the* SCHOOLS SUPERINTENDENT, BOBCHINSKY *and* DOBCHINSKY. *All are in full dress uniform. The scene is conducted in a whisper.*

JUDGE. For pity's sake gentlemen, [get a move on,] get into order . . . tallest in the middle, that's right, it's all got to look right and proper, this here's a man visits the Palace ten times a day, remember, tells off the Privy Council, God help us. Stand to attention, dress by the right . . . no, Peter Ivanovich, you go down that end and you, Peter Ivanovich, up this end. There!

    BOBCHINSKY *and* DOBCHINSKY *scurry on tiptoe to their places.*

CHARITY COMMISSIONER. [That's all very well, Amos Fyodorovich, but] I think we ought to make some sort of move . . . do something.

JUDGE. What sort of move?

CHARITY COMMISSIONER. You know what I mean.

JUDGE (*rubbing finger and thumb together*). A bit of . . . ?

CHARITY COMMISSIONER. Why not?

JUDGE. Too dangerous, that's why not. He's an important man, he might raise an awful stink. Though I suppose we could make it look like a – a public subscription for some monument or other?

POSTMASTER. Couldn't we say it was money that came through the post, and has never been collected?

CHARITY COMMISSIONER. You watch he doesn't send you through the post, Ivan Kuzmich – to somewhere cold and far away! No, listen, that's not the way things are done in a well-ordered society. What are we all doing here *together* like this, eh? We ought to be paying our respects one at a time. Then, when we've each got him alone . . . well, no one's any the wiser, are they? That's the way things are done. And I think you ought to go first, Amos Fyodorovich!

JUDGE. Me? Oh, no, it'd be better for you to go first, he's already broken bread with you, remember.

CHARITY COMMISSIONER. That's exactly why I shouldn't go first. No, I think it should be Luka Lukich. After all, he represents knowledge and enlightenment and that.

SCHOOLS SUPERINTENDENT. I couldn't. No, gentlemen, really, I couldn't! [It's my training.] Soon as anyone even a single grade above me starts speaking, I curl up inside from fright and swallow my tongue! No, I'm sorry, gentlemen, you'll have to excuse me, I can't do it!

CHARITY COMMISSIONER. Well, then, it'll just have to be you, Amos Fyodorovich. You're the one with the silver tongue, you speak just like Cicero.

JUDGE. Cicero, indeed! Just because I get a bit worked up when we're talking about shooting . . .

ALL. Not just shooting . . . !
    You can talk about anything . . . !
    You can do it, Amos Fyodorovich . . . !
    Don't let us down . . . !
    Yes, yes, you must be first . . . !

JUDGE. Please, let me alone, gentlemen! Please!

At this moment there are sounds from the room where KHLYESTAKOV *is sleeping. They all scramble for the door, trampling each other as they go.*

ALL. [Ow, Peter Ivanovich! That's my toe . . . !
    Careful, you're killing me . . . !
    Let me out . . . I'm being squashed to death . . . !
    Ouch . . . ! Help . . . ! Let me through . . . !
    At last the stage is empty.]
    Enter, very slowly, a sleepy KHLYESTAKOV.

KHLYESTAKOV. Whew, what a sleep, I must have been out for hours! Where do they get these feather beds, I wonder? I'm roasted alive! God knows what they gave me to drink yesterday – my head's still buzzing like a hornet's nest. . . . Still, it looks as if I could have a good time here, they're all very hospitable and they seem to do it out of pure kindness of heart, which makes a nice change. . . . That girl, the daughter, isn't a bad little chick . . . and I wouldn't be surprised if the old hen herself had a squawk left in her . . . hmm . . . yes, I must say I rather fancy life in this place.

Enter the JUDGE.

JUDGE (*hovering by the door; aside*). God help me, my knees are giving way!

He draws himself up and puts his hand on his sword.

I have the honour of introducing myself, Your Excellency. Lyapkin-Tyapkin, Civil Captain First Class, Commissioner for Oaths, Judge of the District Court of this town!

KHLYESTAKOV. Ah . . . is that so? Well – er – sit down, won't you? So you're the Judge here, are you?

JUDGE. Elected in 1816 for a three-year term, Your Honour. I have held the post ever since.

KHLYESTAKOV. Really? Quite a – profitable post, I suppose – being Judge in a place like this?

JUDGE (*embarrassed*). After nine years, sir, I was awarded the Order of St Vladimir, Fourth Class. (*Aside.*) Dear God, the money's burning a hole in my hand!

KHLYESTAKOV. I like the Vladimir ribbon – much prettier than the St Anne, don't you think . . . ?

JUDGE (*advancing his fist a little*). God a'mercy, I feel like a cat on hot bricks!

KHLYESTAKOV. What's that you've got in your hand?

JUDGE (*jumps, dropping the notes*). What! Nothing! No, nothing at all!

KHLYESTAKOV. Nothing? But you've dropped a lot of money!

JUDGE (*shaking all over*). Oh – er – no – er – not at all! (*Aside.*) Oh, my God, now I've done it!

KHLYESTAKOV (*picking up the money*). You have, you know. It's money, look!

JUDGE (*aside*). I'm lost – done for – finished!

KHLYESTAKOV. Look here, Judge, I wonder if you'd mind lending me this . . . just a short loan . . . ?

JUDGE (*quickly*). Oh, of course, of course, with pleasure, sir! (*Aside.*) Holy Mary, I'm saved!

KHLYESTAKOV. What with one thing and another I find my travels have run me short of ready money . . . I'll let you have it back, of course, as soon as I reach my estate.

JUDGE. Please, please, Your Honour, don't give it a thought, it's a pleasure, it's a . . . I – I do my best, Your Honour, to serve . . . obey . . . as far as lies . . . as far as I lie . . . as far as in me lies . . . to serve . . . (*He staggers up from his chair and stands to attention.*) I will not disgrace Your Excellency's presence any longer. Does Your Excellency have any instructions for me?

KHLYESTAKOV. Instructions?

JUDGE. About the District Court?

KHLYESTAKOV. Good Lord, no! Why should I . . . (*He thinks.*) No, there's no instructions. Not just now, anyway. Thanks all the same.

JUDGE. (*bowing and scraping his way out; aside*). God be praised, the battle's won! (*He goes off.*)

KHLYESTAKOV. Seems quite a civil fellow – for a Judge.

Enter the POSTMASTER, *rigidly erect, his hand tight on his sword.*

POSTMASTER. I have the honour, sir, to present myself: Shpyokin, Civil Officer Sixth Class and Postmaster.

KHLYESTAKOV. Pleased to meet you, I'm sure. Do sit down. Well – er – I suppose you've always lived around here, have you?

POSTMASTER. That's right, sir.

KHLYESTAKOV. I must say, I like the place. It's not very big, of course, but then it's not supposed to be a capital city, is it? No . . .

POSTMASTER. No, sir. That's quite right, sir.

KHLYESTAKOV. Of course, it's only in the capital that you find the *bon ton* – and can avoid all these dreary provincials. Isn't that so?

POSTMASTER. Oh, yes, yes, indeed, certainly! (*Aside.*) He's not a bit snobbish . . . wants my opinion about everything!

KHLYESTAKOV. Still, there's no reason why people shouldn't be happy even in a small town, is there?

POSTMASTER. No. Er – no, sir, quite correct.

KHLYESTAKOV. I mean – what do people need? Really *need*, to be happy? They just want to be liked and respected by their fellow men, don't they? Anyway, that's what I think.

POSTMASTER. You're absolutely right, Your Honour.

KHLYESTAKOV. I'm delighted you agree. You know, lots of people think I'm a bit odd, but there, that's the way I am. (*Aside.*) Wonder if I can touch this one for a loan, too? (*Aloud.*) D'you know, the oddest thing happened to me the other day. At the last town I stopped at I lost absolutely *all* my money! Every single kopek! Imagine! I suppose you couldn't by any chance lend me three hundred roubles, could you?

POSTMASTER. What? Oh, yes, certainly, with the greatest of pleasure. There you are, sir – three hundred. Very happy to be of service, Your Honour.

KHLYESTAKOV. Very grateful, old chap. I hate running myself short when I'm travelling, don't you know. Anyway, why should I, eh? Why should I?

POSTMASTER. No, indeed, sir, absolutely! (*He draws himself up stiffly.*) I won't trouble Your Excellency any further . . . unless Your Honour has some instructions . . . ?

KHLYESTAKOV. No, no, none at all, old chap.

(*The* POSTMASTER *bows himself out, muttering 'Thank you, Your Honour, thank you, thank you . . .'*)

The Postmaster seems to be a decent sort of chap too. Most obliging. (*He counts his takings.*)

The SCHOOLS SUPERINTENDENT *is shoved into the room, shaking like a leaf; he masters himself, clutches his sword, and advances.*

SCHOOLS SUPERINTENDENT (*gabbling*). Beg the honour introduce self – Khlopov Civil Off. Sec. Class, Super-'ten' Schools!

KHLYESTAKOV. Ah, good, delighted! Sit down, sit down! Have a cigar, old chap?

SCHOOLS SUPERINTENDENT (*aside*). Oh, God, do I take it
. . . or don't I?

KHLYESTAKOV. Come on, come on, take it! It's not a bad one
– nothing to the ones we get in Petersburg, of course, – I
pay twenty-five roubles a hundred for mine, but they're
worth every kopek. Here, light up! (*He offers a light; the*
SCHOOLS SUPERINTENDENT *is trembling so much he can't
get the cigar near the flame.*) That's the wrong end, old boy.
The SCHOOLS SUPERINTENDENT, *panic-stricken, drops the
cigar.*

I can see you're no cigar-lover, old chap.

SCHOOLS SUPERINTENDENT (*aside*). Oh, migawd, I've
ruined everything now!

KHLYESTAKOV. They're one of my weaknesses, I'm afraid.
The other one is (*He leans forward.*) – women! Ah! I just
can't resist a pretty woman! How about you, eh? What
d'you fancy – blondes or brunettes, eh? Oh, come on
now . . .

SCHOOLS SUPERINTENDENT. I daren't venture to have an
opinion, Your Honour.

KHLYESTAKOV. Don't try to wriggle out of it, now! I want to
know!

SCHOOLS SUPERINTENDENT. If I may make so bold, sir,
perhaps . . . I might venture to suggest . . . (*Aside.*) God
Almighty, what am I talking about . . . ?

KHLYESTAKOV. You won't tell me, will you? I think it's those
little brunettes that you fancy, isn't it? Come on now, own
up, you do! (*The* SCHOOLS SUPERINTENDENT *is speechless.*)
Ha! You're blushing! Yes, you are! I was right, wasn't I?
Why wouldn't you say?

SCHOOLS SUPERINTENDENT. I was . . . overawed . . . Your
Excel . . . Your Hon . . . Excellency . . . (*Aside.*) Oh, this
damned tongue of mine!

KHLYESTAKOV. Overawed, eh? Yes, well, there is something
about me that inspires awe, I'm often being told that. There
isn't a woman in the world can hold out against me when
I'm really trying, do you know that?

SCHOOLS SUPERINTENDENT. I'm sure they can't, sir.

KHLYESTAKOV. Yes. Well. Look – er – something damned awkward's happened to me. On my way here I somehow managed to run out of cash completely . . . you don't happen to be able to lend me three hundred roubles, do you?

SCHOOLS SUPERINTENDENT (*searching his pockets feverishly; aside*). Oh, God, I've lost it, I've lost it . . . ! No, here it is! (*To* KHLYESTAKOV.) There! Three hundred!

He hands over the notes, shaking with fear.

KHLYESTAKOV. Splendid. Thanks a lot.

SCHOOLS SUPERINTENDENT (*stands, clutching his sword*). I won't impose on Your Honour a moment longer. Except to say . . . to say . . . to say . . .

KHLYESTAKOV (*counting the notes*). Goodbye, then!

SCHOOLS SUPERINTENDENT (*aside, as he scuttles out*). Thank God for that! With a bit of luck he won't want to look at the school at all! (*He goes off.*)

Enter the CHARITY COMMISSIONER, *erect and bland.*

CHARITY COMMISSIONER. May I have the honour of presenting myself, Your Excellency? Zemlyanika, Civil Captain Third Class and Commissioner of Charities.

KHLYESTAKOV. How d'you do? Sit down, please.

CHARITY COMMISSIONER. I had the great honour and pleasure of receiving Your Excellency at the hospital yesterday, [and of showing you personally round the charitable institutions in my charge.]

KHLYESTAKOV. So you did. That was an excellent lunch you gave me, too!

CHARITY COMMISSIONER. I am happy at all times to put myself at the service of my country.

KHLYESTAKOV. Good food is a weakness of mine, you know. (*He looks at the* CHARITY COMMISSIONER *closely.*) You know, you seem a bit taller today than you were yesterday.

CHARITY COMMISSIONER. That's quite possible. (*A brief silence.*) I never spare myself, sir, when serving the state. (*Another silence. He inches his chair forward.*) Which is more than can be said, I'm afraid, for the Postmaster. He never does a stroke. Everything gets held up, letters, documents, everything . . . ! And the Judge – [he uses that courtroom of his as a kennel!] He may be a relation of mine but I must say his general conduct is really scandalous! Scandalous!

KHLYESTAKOV. Is that a fact?

CHARITY COMMISSIONER (*coming closer*). There's a land-owner here, name of Dobchinsky – [Your Excellency saw him yesterday, I think] – soon as this poor Dobchinsky leaves his house, that Judge pops straight in the back door to see Dobchinsky's wife! True as I sit here, sir! Not one of those little Dobchinsky children looks like Dobchinsky, you'll see that for yourself! Every one of 'em, even the little girl, poor thing, looks like the Judge!

KHLYESTAKOV. Is that so? I'd never have thought it of him!

CHARITY COMMISSIONER (*closer still*). And that Superintend-ent of Schools . . . it's a total mystery how that one got himself appointed! Why, he's no better than an anarchist, and that school of his is a hotbed of revolution. If Your Excellency so desires, I'll put all this down in writing.

KHLYESTAKOV. Yes, you do that, will you? I like to have something amusing to read when I'm bored. What did you say your name was?

CHARITY COMMISSIONER. Zemlyanika.

KHLYESTAKOV. Ah, yes. (*Pause.*) Do you have any children?

CHARITY COMMISSIONER. I have five, Your Excellency, [– two already grown up.

KHLYESTAKOV. Two grown up? Really? And – er – what are they – er?

CHARITY COMMISSIONER. Their names, Your Excellency?] Nikolai, Ivan, Elizabeta, Marya and Perpetua!

KHLYESTAKOV. Oh, splendid! Congratulations!

CHARITY COMMISSIONER. I won't take up any more of your time, Your Excellency . . . (*Rising.*) I'm sure you have more urgent duties . . . (*Bowing himself out.*)

KHLYESTAKOV. Not at all, not at all, it's all been most interesting, you must come and have another chat with me some time, I'm extremely fond of . . . (*The* CHARITY COMMISSIONER *is fast vanishing.*) Oh – er – what did you say your name was?

CHARITY COMMISSIONER. Artemy Philipovich Zemlyanika.

KHLYESTAKOV. Well, look here, Artemy Philipovich, the damnedest thing's happened to me – I've been cleaned out of cash . . . cleaned right out! I suppose you couldn't lend me – er – say, four hundred . . . ?

CHARITY COMMISSIONER (*resigned*). Here you are. Three . . . four hundred.

KHLYESTAKOV. Oh, I say, isn't that lucky? Thank you so much, my dear chap!

    The CHARITY COMMISSIONER *goes off.*

    Enter BOBCHINSKY *and* DOBCHINSKY.

BOBCHINSKY. I have the honour of introducing myself – Peter Ivanovich Bobchinsky, resident of this town and landowner.

DOBCHINSKY. Peter Ivanovich Dobchinsky, landowner and – er – resident of this town.

KHLYESTAKOV. I've met you both, haven't I? (*To* BOBCHIN-SKY.) [Aren't you the one that fell through the door?] How's your nose today?

BOBCHINSKY. Please don't concern yourself, Excellency. God be praised, it's quite healed.

KHLYESTAKOV. I'm delighted to hear it. (*He suddenly rounds on them.*) Have you got any money on you?

DOBCHINSKY. Money?

BOBCHINSKY. Money!

KHLYESTAKOV. A thousand roubles or so. As a loan.

BOBCHINSKY. A thousand? Before God, Your Excellency, I've nothing like that! Have you, Peter Ivanovich?

DOBCHINSKY. Certainly not. All my money's in State Bonds, I assure you.

KHLYESTAKOV. Well, if you haven't a thousand, can you let me have a hundred?

BOBCHINSKY (*fumbling in his pockets*). Haven't you got a hundred roubles, Peter Ivanovich? All I've got is forty.

DOBCHINSKY (*searching*). I've got twenty-five.

BOBCHINSKY. Have another look. I know you've got a hole in your righthand pocket – something may have slipped down into the lining.

DOBCHINSKY (*feeling*). There's nothing there, I'm afraid.

KHLYESTAKOV. Don't bother, please, I just thought I'd ask. Sixty-five will do for the moment ... (*He takes it.*)

DOBCHINSKY. Er-hum. Sir. I wish to take the liberty of asking your advice in a very – um – delicate matter.

KHLYESTAKOV. Ask away, old chap.

DOBCHINSKY. It's – er – very delicate. My son, do you see, was born to me before my marriage.

KHLYESTAKOV. Yes ...?

DOBCHINSKY (*embarrassed*). Well, in a manner of speaking, that is. It's just that we had – er – part of the marriage before the marriage, if you follow, sir. [Then afterwards, of course, it was made proper, the full ties of matrimony and everything.] But I want my son to have my name – Dobchinsky – instead of his mother's, do you see?

KHLYESTAKOV. Naturally. There's no difficulty, is there? Let him be called Dobchinsky!

DOBCHINSKY. I wouldn't bother you with this, Excellency, except he's such a very gifted boy! [He knows lots of poems by heart, and only let him get hold of a knife, he does the most remarkable carvings.] Isn't that so, Peter Ivanovich?

BOBCHINSKY. He's very talented, Excellency.

KHLYESTAKOV. Good, delighted to hear it! I'll put in a word for you in the proper quarters. Yes, yes, yes ... (*He turns to* BOBCHINSKY.) And is there anything I can do for you?

BOBCHINSKY. Yes, indeed, Excellency. A humble request.

KHLYESTAKOV. Well? What is it?

BOBCHINSKY. When you go back to Petersburg, Excellency, I humbly beg you should say to these grand people, these admirals and senators and that, say to them, 'Your Grace ... your Serenity ...' or whatever it is '... in this little town there lives a man called Peter Ivanovich Bobchinsky!' Just you tell them that: 'There lives a man called Peter Ivanovich Bobchinsky!'

KHLYESTAKOV. All right.

BOBCHINSKY. And if you should happen to meet the Tsar, Excellency, you say to him, 'Do you know, Your Imperial Majesty, in this little town there lives a man called Peter Ivanovich Bobchinsky!'

KHLYESTAKOV. All right.

DOBCHINSKY. Please excuse us for bothering you with our presence.

BOBCHINSKY. Please excuse us for bothering you with our presence.

KHLYESTAKOV. Not at all, it's been a pleasure. (*He shows them out.*) All these poor boobies seem to have taken me for some sort of Government official. I must have spun them a hell of a line yesterday. What an army of dimwits! I must write and tell Tryapichkin about them. He could put them into one of those funny articles of his . . . Hey! Ossip!

He begins writing the letter – saying the words as he writes them:

'My dear Tryapichkin, the most extraordinary things have been happening to me . . .' (*He giggles.*) . . . What a laugh! Just let Tryapichkin get his teeth into this lot. He's a man wouldn't spare his own father to make a good joke. One thing about all these fools, they're good-natured. All this cash! Let's see, now . . . three hundred from that Judge, another three from the Postmaster . . . six, seven, eight hundred . . . agh, what a filthy note! . . . my life, that's over a thousand! Just let me meet that rotten infantry captain again, I'll take him . . . !

Enter OSSIP.

Well, stupid, you see how these people receive me, eh? (*He goes on writing.*)

OSSIP (*sees the money*). Yes, sir, praise be to God. But may I say something, Ivan Alexandrovich?

KHLYESTAKOV. Hm?

OSSIP. The sooner we skip, the better. We best be gone soon.

KHLYESTAKOV (*keeps on writing*). Nonsense! Why?

OSSIP. [That's the way it is, sir. God bless 'em.] They've given us two good days, that's as much as we can expect. No point in hanging about . . . let's get out while we can. [Our luck'll change if we don't, sir, you mark my words.] They've got some lovely horses here; we could be away like the wind.

KHLYESTAKOV (*writing*). I want to stay a bit longer, Ossip. Perhaps we'll go tomorrow.

OSSIP. Tomorrow's too late! Honest to God, sir, why don't we go now? They're making a fine old fuss of you at the moment, but that's all on account of they've mistaken you for some sort of high official from Petersburg.

KHLYESTAKOV. I know!

OSSIP. It can't last. And your father isn't half going to be wild with you taking so long to get home! They've got these lovely horses here, it'd be a shame to waste 'em!

KHLYESTAKOV. All right, all right, all right! But I want this letter to go off first, you can order your lovely horses at the same time. [See we get the best, Ossip! Tell the drivers I'll give them each a silver rouble if they drive like gods and sing like angels . . .] (*He goes on writing.*) Tryapichkin's going to die laughing when he reads this . . .

OSSIP. I'll get one of the men here to take it, sir. I'd best start on the packing.

KHLYESTAKOV. All right. But bring me a candle, Ossip.

OSSIP (*going out – off*). Hey! You! We've got a letter here for the post. [You can tell the Postmaster it doesn't need a stamp, it's official. And tell the stables to send round the best horses they've got – express team. Tell 'em they needn't worry about the money, the Ministry pays. And tell 'em to get moving, or my master'll be angry! All right, hold on then, the letter's not ready yet.]

KHLYESTAKOV (*writing*). Where's he living now? Is it still Post Office Street? He flits about so much . . . cheaper than paying rent, I suppose. . . . Oh, I'll chance it . . . (*Addressing the letter.*) 'Tryapichkin, Post Office Street . . .'

OSSIP *brings a candle, and* KHLYESTAKOV *seals his letter. He gives it to* OSSIP.

There you are.

The voices of the SHOPKEEPERS *are heard off.*

DYERZHIMORDA (*off*). [Hey, who d'you think you're shoving? I've got orders not to let anyone in here!]

SHOPKEEPERS (*off*). Let us in!

You can't keep us out!

We're going in!

We've got business here . . . !

DYERZHIMORDA (*off*). Move along now, come on, he's not seeing anybody now. He's asleep. Move along there, please!

The noise gets worse.

KHLYESTAKOV. What's all the noise, Ossip? [See what's going on, will you?]

OSSIP. There's a lot of people trying to get in, all waving bits of paper. I think it's you they want to see.

KHLYESTAKOV (*going to the window*). Well, my friends, what is it? What do you want?

SHOPKEEPERS (*off*). We appeal to Your Excellency!

Tell them to let us through!

We have a petition, Your Honour!

KHLYESTAKOV. Let 'em in! Let 'em all in! Go on, Ossip, go and tell the constable to let them come in!

OSSIP *goes off.*

KHLYESTAKOV (*receives petitions through the window*). 'To His Most Noble Reverence, the Master of Finance [from Abdullin General Stores and Grain merchant . . .'] Master of Finance . . . there's no such title! What the devil's all this about?

OSSIP *shepherds in the* SHOPKEEPERS.

Well, my friends, what can I do for you?

FIRST SHOPKEEPER. We humbly beg your gracious favour, noble lord!

SECOND SHOPKEEPER. Don't let us be ruined, Your Honour!

THIRD SHOPKEEPER. Save us from this oppression, Your Highness!

KHLYESTAKOV. Who's oppressing you?

ABDULLIN. It's the Mayor, Your Honour! There's never been a Mayor like him, that's a fact. [A man can't tell the things that Mayor'll do to us poor tradesmen. He billets the soldiers on us till we're all but ruined. He insults every last one of us. He pulls our beards and calls us peasants and gypsies. It's not right, Your Honour.] We're respectable citizens, we always do what's needed, he gets what's his due

[– none of us'll kick at handing over a bit of cloth for his wife or his daughter,] but sir, that man's never satisfied! He'll walk into your shop and take the first thing his eye lights on. 'That's a nice bit of cloth,' he'll say, 'send it round to my place . . .' And of course we have to send it round!

KHLYESTAKOV. Tst, tst, tst! What a scoundrel, eh?

FIRST SHOPKEEPER. [No one can remember a Mayor like him, Your Honour.] We have to hide everything in the shop, soon as we see him coming! [T'in't as if it was only the delicacies he was after.] Nothing's safe from him! [Some rubbishy old prunes as've been mouldering in the barrel these past seven year, what no errand boy'd look at, he'll shove his great fist in that barrel.

SECOND SHOPKEEPER. We're generous enough to him on his name day, Your Honour, but that one's not satisfied with one name day, he has to celebrate every Saint in the calendar, so he do!

KHLYESTAKOV. He sounds like a regular brigand!

THIRD SHOPKEEPER. So he is, sir!]

ABDULLIN. But we don't dare complain, Your Honour. He'll billet a whole regiment on you if he finds out, or close down your business. ['I can't have you flogged or tortured,' he'll say, 'that's against the law, but I can see you eat nothing but salt herrings for the rest of your life!']

KHLYESTAKOV. The man's a monster! He ought to be sent straight to Siberia!

ABDULLIN. Ah, that'd do, or anywhere else Your Excellency likes to send him, just so's it's a long way off! Now, sir, Your Excellency won't scorn our humble offerings . . . just this sack of sugar here, and a basket of wine . . .

KHLYESTAKOV. I'm sorry, I couldn't possibly accept them – what can you be thinking of me! I never accept bribes, my friends! However . . . I seem to be a little short of cash . . . if you happened to be in a position to make me a small loan . . . say three hundred roubles . . . a loan is something I can accept.

ALL. Of course, by all means!

Please accept more, Your Excellency!

Take five hundred, sir . . .

. . . just to please us!

KHLYESTAKOV. Well, I've nothing against a small loan, thank you, thank you . . .

ABDULLIN *offers the money on a silver salver.*

ABDULLIN. Please, Your Honour, won't you take the salver as well?

KHLYESTAKOV. If you insist, I suppose I could take that.

SECOND SHOPKEEPER (*bowing*). Won't you take the sugar too, Your Honour?

KHLYESTAKOV. I'm sorry. I can't accept bribes . . .

OSSIP. Oh, come on, why not, Your Honour? A bit of sugar can come in very handy on the road, you know. Here, I'll take them, put the sugar over here, and the wine. . . . What's that you got there? A bit of rope, is it – here, let's have that too, rope's always useful when you're travelling, for lashing things up and so on . . .

ABDULLIN. Please help us, Your Serenity! If you don't do anything about the Mayor after all this, we might as well all drown ourselves, we'll be finished for good!

KHLYESTAKOV. Of course, my friends, of course, I'll do everything I can!

The SHOPKEEPERS *go off. A* WOMAN'S *voice is heard, off.*

VOICE. That's enough of your pushing, now! I'll tell His Excellency on you! Stop shoving, you're hurting!

KHLYESTAKOV. Who's that now? (*He goes to the window.*) What is it, woman, what's the trouble?

VOICES OF TWO WOMEN. Mercy, Your Honour!

Give us a hearing, sir!

Tell them to let us in!

Etc. . . .

KHLYESTAKOV. [Let them in then, Constable.]

The LOCKSMITH'S WIFE *and the* SERGEANT'S WIDOW *enter.*

LOCKSMITH'S WIFE (*bowing to the floor*). Have mercy on us, Your Honour!

SERGEANT'S WIDOW (*same bow*). Have mercy on us, Your Honour!

KHLYESTAKOV. Why? Who are you?

LOCKSMITH'S WIFE. Petrova Poshlyopkin, my husband's the locksmith, he was . . .

SERGEANT'S WIDOW. Ivanovna, the Sergeant's widow. I was . . .

KHLYESTAKOV. Wait a minute, one at a time! (*To the* LOCKSMITH'S WIFE.) Now then, what is it?

LOCKSMITH'S WIFE. It's the Mayor, Your Honour, God rot him. [I pray God to fill his whole filthy family with pesky diseases, all his children and brothers and uncles and aunts and the whole rotten lot of them, may they all stink in hell!

KHLYESTAKOV. Why? What on earth has he done?]

LOCKSMITH'S WIFE. Sent my husband off to the army, that's what, your Honour! And him a married man, that's against the law!

KHLYESTAKOV. [How could he do that, then?

LOCKSMITH'S WIFE. Oh, he could do it, all right, the lousy hog, may God blast him with boils in this world and the next! May his flesh drop off with the plague, and his aunt's filthy flesh too, and his rotten father's stinking flesh too, if he's got a father, which I doubt, please God let them all die horribly and burn forever in hell.] He should have taken that tailor's son, [he's nothing but a nasty little drunk,] only his parents could afford a nice big bribe, [so he picks on the draper's son instead but she – that's his mother, she's a widow – sends three bolts of good linen to the Mayor's wife, so then he comes to me. 'What good's a husband to you,' he says, 'he's no more use as a husband,' he says. 'Well,' says I, 'that's my business whether he's any use or not, I'm the only one as knows that,' I says. 'But he's a thief,' he says, 'perhaps he hasn't stolen anything yet,' he says, 'but he will soon,' he says, 'and then he'll be sent for a soldier anyway,' he says.] I'm only a woman, Your Honour, what'll I do without a man around the house?

KHLYESTAKOV. All right, all right, that'll do . . . !

LOCKSMITH'S WIFE. [Please, sir, don't desert us, please do something . . .]

KHLYESTAKOV (*to the* SERGEANT'S WIDOW). And what about you, then?

SERGEANT'S WIDOW. It's the Mayor, sir.

KHLYESTAKOV. Yes, of course. But what about him?

SERGEANT'S WIDOW. He had me flogged, sir.

KHLYESTAKOV (*interested*). Really?

SERGEANT'S WIDOW. [It was all wrong, Your Honour. Some of the women was fighting in the market, and the police didn't get there 'til it was all over. And that man picked on me for no reason, he had them give me such a thrashing] I couldn't sit down for two days, Your Honour!

KHLYESTAKOV. I don't see I can do much about that now.

The SERGEANT'S WIDOW *and the* LOCKSMITH'S WIFE *speak together.*

SERGEANT'S WIDOW. I know you can't undo what's done, Your Honour, but you could make that rascal pay me damages, couldn't you? I don't have much luck, Your Honour, I might as well try where I can . . . a few roubles would come in very handy just now . . .

LOCKSMITH'S WIFE. That stinking swindling louse, I hope all his children and his grandchildren die at birth and if he's got any in-laws, God make them die slowly . . .

KHLYESTAKOV (*shutting them up*). Very well! I'll see to it, don't worry! . . . You can run along now . . . (*He shoos them out.*)

Hands holding petitions are thrust through the window. Hubbub outside.

What the hell's happening out there? (*He goes to the window.*) No, I don't want them, take them away! Go away all of you, I don't want your petitions! (*He leaves the window.*) Ossip, get rid of them, for God's sake, I'm sick of the lot of them! Don't let any more in! (*At the window.*) All right, shove off, the lot of you. Go on, buzz! Come back tomorrow!

The door opens and a battered man in a shabby coat, his lip swollen and his face bandaged, unshaven, miserable, hovers in the entrance; behind him, many more similar figures can be seen.

OSSIP. Here, outside, you! Come on, out!

> OSSIP *shoves the man back into the crowd and follows him out, closing the door behind him. Enter, from the inner door,* MARIA.

KHLYESTAKOV (*calling off*). Ossip! The horses!

MARIA (*girlishly startled*). Oh!

KHLYESTAKOV. Why so frightened, may I ask?

MARIA. I wasn't frightened, really . . .

KHLYESTAKOV. Allow me to say, dear lady, I would be delighted to think you might have thought I would think that you . . . hrchm . . . (*Striking an attitude.*) May I ask where you were going?

MARIA. Why, I wasn't going anywhere, really.

KHLYESTAKOV. And why were you not going anywhere, really, dear lady?

MARIA. I thought perhaps Mamma was in here.

KHLYESTAKOV. Of course. But your real reason . . . ?

MARIA (*hedging*). I'm being a nuisance. I'm sure you've got some awfully important business to attend to.

KHLYESTAKOV (*posturing again*). What business could ever be as important to me, dear lady, as looking into your incomparable eyes? You couldn't possibly be a nuisance, your presence could only be a pleasure!

MARIA. The way you talk! Just like real society!

KHLYESTAKOV. To such a gorgeous creature as yourself, how else should I talk? May I have the extreme happiness of offering you a chair? Only you should have not a simple chair, but a throne!

MARIA. I don't know. I think I ought to be going. (*But she sits down.*)

KHLYESTAKOV. What a beautiful scarf you're wearing!

MARIA. Oh! Go on, you're making fun of me! Just because I'm a provincial . . . !

KHLYESTAKOV. How I would love to be that scarf, nestling so closely round your lily-white neck.

MARIA. What are you talking about? Wanting to be a scarf . . . ! What strange weather we're having today.

KHLYESTAKOV. Your lips, dear lady, are stranger and more inscrutably fascinating than any weather!

MARIA. [Really, the things you say!] Won't you write some verses for my album – I'm sure you know lots of verses, don't you?

KHLYESTAKOV. For you – I could do anything. Ask, and it will be done! What sort of verses would you like?

MARIA. Something . . . well, you know, something good. Something new.

KHLYESTAKOV. Oh, verses, verses . . . I know so many of them!

MARIA. Won't you recite some, then?

KHLYESTAKOV. But why? I can write them down without all that.

MARIA. I'm fond of listening to poems. . . .

KHLYESTAKOV. Well, I know dozens of them, dozens.

MARIA. Well, go on!

KHLYESTAKOV. Well, if you insist, here's one of mine I might put in your album –
    'Shall I compare thee to a summer's day?
    Thou art more lovely and more temperate;
    Rough winds do shake de dum de dum de dum.'
And so on and so forth – that's one of my sonnets. I've done lots more, lots, I just can't remember the words this instant. Oh, but what do poems matter, I'd much rather speak of the love I feel when I gaze into your beautiful eyes . . . (*He draws his chair closer to hers.*)

MARIA. Love! Oh, I don't know anything about that. [I don't even know what the word means. . . .] (*She edges her chair away.*)

KHLYESTAKOV (*moving up again*). Why do you move away? It's much nicer being close together!

MARIA (*moving away*). I think it's nicer (*She shifts.*) further (*She shifts.*) away.

KHLYESTAKOV (*closer*). But there's no need to move away. You only imagine we're close. You could just as well imagine we're far apart. Ah, but how happy I would be, dear lady, if I could enfold you in my arms . . .

MARIA (*looking suddenly out of the window*). Oh, look! What sort of bird was that? Was it a magpie?

KHLYESTAKOV (*kissing her shoulder*). Here's a magpie!

MARIA (*jumping up indignantly*). No, really, that's too much!

KHLYESTAKOV (*holding her back*). Forgive me, Ma'am, please forgive me! It was only my great love made me do it, only my love . . .

MARIA. You think just because I'm a country girl you can . . . (*She tries to get away.*)

KHLYESTAKOV (*still holding her*). No! It was love, I swear to you, I meant no harm, it was only my unconquerable love! Oh, forgive me, forgive me, Maria Antonovna, I'll go down on my knees to you if you'll forgive me! (*He falls on his knees.*) Look, look, I'm on my knees before you!

Enter ANNA ANDREYEVNA.

ANNA. Well! This is a surprise! (*To* MARIA.) What does all this mean, then? That's a fine way to behave, I'm sure!

MARIA. Really, Mamma, it wasn't . . .

ANNA. Leave the room this instant! Go on, run along! And don't you dare show your face in here again! (MARIA *goes off in tears.*) I'm sorry, Your Honour, but really – well, it *was* rather a surprise!

KHLYESTAKOV (*aside*). She's quite fetching herself – hm, hm, not bad at all . . . (*He shuffles towards her on his knees.*) Oh, Madame, Madame, can't you see that I'm dying of love!

ANNA. Oh, do get up, sir, the floor's filthy!

KHLYESTAKOV. No, no, on my knees . . . I must stay on my knees . . . 'til I hear my fate. . . . Is it to be life . . . or death?

ANNA. I don't know what you're carrying on about, really I don't. Are you making a declaration about my daughter?

KHLYESTAKOV. No, no, it's you I'm in love with, you! My whole life is at stake, for if you can't return my undying love then I'm not worthy of life at all! My heart is on fire as I beg for your hand . . . !

ANNA. But sir, I must point out that I am – er – in a manner of speaking – er – married.

KHLYESTAKOV. Married! What is marriage! True love knows

nothing of these formalities! As the poet said – ''Tis but itself the law condemns!'

ANNA. They do say 'True love can leap the fastest torrent', don't they?

KHLYESTAKOV. Of course it can, beloved lady! We'll fly together, hand in hand, to the banks of some gurgling brook. . . . Your hand, I beg you, your hand!

Enter MARIA, *running.*

MARIA. Mamma, Pappa says you're to . . . (*She cries out as she sees* KHLYESTAKOV *on his knees.*) Well, what a surprise!

ANNA. What are you doing here, you little fidget, dashing in like a scalded cat, I thought I told you to keep out? What's a surprise, eh? I don't know what nonsense you've got in your head now, you're just like a child, no one would guess you were eighteen years old! [Won't you ever learn to behave like a properly brought-up young lady, haven't you got any manners at all?]

MARIA (*in tears*). But Mamma, I didn't know . . .

ANNA. You don't know nothing, that's your trouble, always in a whirl, just like those Lyapkin-Tyapkin girls, can't you find a better model than them? You could take your mother as an example, for instance, couldn't you?

KHLYESTAKOV (*taking* MARIA'*s hand*). Anna Andreyevna, I beg you not to oppose our happiness! Give your blessing to our love!

ANNA (*astonished*). What? You mean – it's *her*?

Heavy winking from KHLYESTAKOV.

KHLYESTAKOV. Tell me quickly – is it life – or death?

ANNA (*turning on* MARIA). There, you see, you stupid girl? Just for the sake of a silly little baggage like you, His Excellency has to go down on his knees to me! And then of course you have to burst in like a lunatic . . . it would serve you right if I said no, just to teach you a lesson. You don't deserve such luck!

MARIA. I won't do it again, Mamma, I promise.

Enter MAYOR, *breathless.*

MAYOR. Your Excellency, mercy! Have mercy on me!

KHLYESTAKOV. Now what's the matter?

MAYOR. Those shopkeepers have been making complaints about me, I know they have, and it's all lies, not half of it's true, they're cheats and liars, the lot of them, they're always giving short measure and that. And that Sergeant's widow said I had her flogged; it's a rotten lie, she flogged herself!

KHLYESTAKOV. Oh, to hell with the Sergeant's widow, I've got other things to think about!

MARIA. Pappa, His Excellency has asked . . .

MAYOR. Don't you believe a word of it, Your Honour! They're just a pack of rotten liars! [A baby could see through them, the whole town knows what liars they are. And swindle – they'd swindle their own mothers out of half a kopek and boast about it, Your Honour!]

MARIA. Pappa, I think His Excellency wants to ask . . .

ANNA. Be quiet, girl! Do you know the honour Ivan Alexandrovich is doing us, my dear? He's asked for our daughter's hand in marriage!

MAYOR. What?! You're out of your mind, woman! Don't be angry with her, Your Excellency, she's a bit weak in the head. Her mother was just the same.

KHLYESTAKOV. But I really am asking your consent to my marrying your daughter. I love her!

MAYOR. I don't believe it.

ANNA. [But His Excellency is telling you!

KHLYESTAKOV. I'm quite serious. I'm going mad with love!

MAYOR. You must be joking.]

ANNA. God Almighty, what a fool the man is! His Excellency is *telling* you, dear!

MAYOR. I can't believe it.

KHLYESTAKOV. You must give us your consent! I'm desperate. I could do something awful if you refuse . . . and then my blood would be on your hands!

MAYOR. No, no, please, I'm innocent, I haven't done a thing; I swear it. . . . Yes, anything Your Excellency pleases. Oh, God! What am I saying? My head's going round! [I don't know what's happening . . . God a'mercy, I'm such a fool!]

ANNA. For pity's sake, give them your blessing, then!

> KHLYESTAKOV *approaches the* MAYOR, *leading* MARIA *by the hand.*

MAYOR. May God bless you both, I suppose, but none of it's my fault, I'm entirely innocent, you know.

> KHLYESTAKOV *kisses* MARIA. *The* MAYOR *is still puzzled.*

Hey, look, they're kissing each other!

> *The* MAYOR *rubs his eyes and stares.*

It's true! Is it true? It's true, they're engaged!

> *The* MAYOR *dances with joy.*

What about that, Anton! Three cheers for the Mayor! What a stroke of genius!

> *Enter* OSSIP.

OSSIP. The horses are ready, sir.

KHLYESTAKOV. Ah . . . right. Coming now.

MAYOR. What's that? Horses? Are you leaving?

KHLYESTAKOV. That's right.

MAYOR. But didn't I understand . . . ? Your Excellency was pleased to hint – er – possible marriage?

KHLYESTAKOV. Oh, I shan't be away a minute, well, that is, no more than a day . . . to see my uncle, you know, very rich uncle, have to get his blessing too, of course. I'll be back tomorrow.

MAYOR. We wouldn't presume to keep you, of course. We can only await the happiness of your return.

KHLYESTAKOV. That's right. Good. Well, I'll be back in no time. Goodbye, my darling . . . oh, I can't find words to express all I feel! Goodbye, beloved, my love, my darling, goodbye . . . (*He kisses* MARIA'S *hand.*)

MAYOR. Is there nothing you need for the road, Your Excellency? You were a little short of ready money . . .

KHLYESTAKOV. No, no, what on earth made you think . . . (*Pause.*) Yes, well, perhaps I am – a bit short.

MAYOR. How much do you need?

KHLYESTAKOV. Let's see now, you lent me two hundred – no, of course, it was four, I mustn't take advantage of your mistake, must I? So if you could just let me have the same again, that would make a round eight hundred, wouldn't it?

MAYOR. Certainly, certainly! (*He produces notes.*) There, all in nice crisp new notes!

KHLYESTAKOV. Really! (*He takes the notes and examines them.*) Very nice, too. They say new banknotes bring you luck, don't they?

MAYOR. Indeed they do.

KHLYESTAKOV. Well, goodbye then, Anton Antonovich. Thanks for all your hospitality. I can say quite sincerely that I've never been so well received – anywhere, ever before, never! Goodbye, Anna Andreyevna! And farewell, my darling Maria Antonovna! (KHLYESTAKOV *and* MARIA *go out together.*) My heart's joy! My angel! Goodbye!

MAYOR (*at the door*). Surely you're not riding in that dreadful public cart?

KHLYESTAKOV (*off*). Really, I prefer it. Springs make my head ache, you know.

DRIVER (*off*). Whoa-up!

MAYOR. At least let me get you something to sit on – a rug or something!

KHLYESTAKOV. What on earth for, it's nothing. (*Pause.*) Well, all right, if you insist.

MAYOR. Avdotya! Fetch a rug from the boxroom – the best one, the Persian rug with the blue border – hurry! (*He goes out.*)

DRIVER (*off*). Whoa!

MAYOR (*off*). When can we expect Your Excellency back?

KHLYESTAKOV (*off*). Tomorrow or the next day.

OSSIP (*off*). Is that our rug? All right, over here with it, tuck it round, that's right. Let's have some of that hay over here, then.

DRIVER (*off*). More hay here, no, over this side, you daft lump, that's it, now the rug, good. There you are, Your Excellency, you'll be nice and comfy.

KHLYESTAKOV (*off*). Goodbye, all! Goodbye, Anton Antonovich.

MAYOR (*off*). }
MARIA (*off*). } Goodbye, Your Excellency.

ANNA (*at window*). Goodbye, Ivan Alexandrovich!

KHLYESTAKOV (*off*). Goodbye, Mamma! Goodbye, Pappa!

DRIVER (*off*). Giddyap, giddyap!

> *The carriage bells ring into the distance.*
>
> *The* MAYOR *returns with* ANNA, *followed a moment later by* MARIA.

MAYOR. Aha, Anna, you never thought anything like this would happen, did you? A fine catch for your daughter, eh? Come on, admit it! [You never dreamed of such a thing, did you?] One moment you're just the wife of the Mayor and then, by damn! Suddenly you've got a young blood like that for a son-in-law!

ANNA. Nonsense, Anton, I knew it all along. It may be a surprise to you, but you're such a peasant, you've never mixed with decent people before.

MAYOR. Decent people! I'm decent people myself, [thank you!] Eh, but just think, Anna – what it does to us, we'll be flying high now, all right. (*He shouts off.*) Hey, you there! Come here! I'll fix that bunch of crooks! I'll teach 'em to come running with their complaints and petitions and that, they'll wish they'd never been born.

> *Enter the* CONSTABLE.

Ah, it's you, Pugovitzin. Run and fetch those shopkeepers back here, sonny! By God, I'll fix that dirty pack of creeping Judases! [They're not going to get away with it this time, I'm going to make their lives hell, sheer burning hell! I want a list of everyone that came here to complain, everyone that signed a petition – yes, and the dirty scribblers who wrote out their petitions for them, put them all on the list!] See that everyone knows exactly how God has chosen to honour their Mayor. [Tell them he's not going to marry his daughter to any rotten common *ordinary* man, he's going to marry her to one of the grandest, one of the most powerful men in the whole world – a man such as they've never met, a man who can do anything, anything!] Tell them all! Shout it from the housetops, ring every bell in the town, damn it, make it a real celebration! Go on, hop it.

> *The* CONSTABLE *goes off.*

So that's the way it's going to be. Well, Anna, where would you like to live – here, or in Petersburg?

ANNA. In Petersburg, of course! We couldn't possibly stay on here.

MAYOR. If you say Petersburg, my dear, Petersburg it shall be. Mind you, I'm not sure it wouldn't be just as nice to stay on here . . . it'll mean the end of my being Mayor, if we leave.

ANNA. I should think so too! There's not much to being a Mayor.

MAYOR. Hey! [D'you think I might get a high-up job in the Service, then, Anna?] With him being a personal friend of all the Ministers, and popping in and out of the Palace and that, he ought to get me promoted easy enough. Perhaps they'll make me a General! Eh, Anna? What do you think? Do you think they'll make me a General?

ANNA. I should hope so, I'm sure.

MAYOR. Dear God, I'd love to be a General! All those decorations across my chest [– which do you like best, Anna, the red for St Anne, or the blue of the White Eagle?

ANNA. The blue, of course.

MAYOR. Ha, you women, you always want the best! Even the red'd be nice, though. You know what's good about being a General, Anna? Everywhere you go there's] all those adjutants and couriers scurrying on ahead demanding the best horses for you. There won't be no horses for nobody else, but they'll have some for the General; the rest just have to wait their turn! . . . Councillors, Captains – yes – ha! And Mayors! They all have to wait! Ah! Those Mayors! Ha-ha! [You go to dine at the Governor's and all those Mayors – ha! they all have to stand up – ha-ha! – and bow – ha-ha! And you just ignore the whole rotten lot of them!] (*He doubles up with laughter and slaps his knees again and again.*) Yes, by damn, that's what I like about being a General!

ANNA. [I never heard anything so coarse, really! You've got to understand, Anton, our life's going to be completely different now, our friends won't be loud-mouthed judges

who can't think about anything but shooting rabbits, they'll
be counts and things, all sorts of society people with lovely
refeened manners. In fact, Anton, I'm a bit worried about
you – you sometimes come out with words and expressions
that are *never* used in polite society!

MAYOR. Ah, to hell with that, words never did anyone any
harm.

ANNA. Not when you're only a Mayor in a little country town,
perhaps. But in Petersburg things are all very different, you
know.

MAYOR. Yes, they say they serve a coulibiac of salmon that
makes you faint at the first taste!

ANNA. A fine time to be talking about fish! In Petersburg . . .
in Petersburg . . . we're going to have the finest house in
town! I shall have my boudoir drenched in the finest
perfume, so people will have to close their eyes in ecstasy as
they come in . . . like this. (*She closes her eyes and sniffs,
swooning.*)]

Enter the SHOPKEEPERS, *sheepishly.*

MAYOR. Aha, there you are, my fine friends!

SHOPKEEPERS (*all bowing low*). We wish you the best of
health, Your Honour.

MAYOR. I bet you do! And how are you all, eh? How's
business? Why, you tea-swillers, you counter-jumpers, you
short-change merchants, so you thought you'd complain
about me did you? You crooks, you creeping two-faced
misbegotten store-rats! Scum! Well? Speak up. Where's it
got you, eh? Thought you'd get me behind bars, did you?
[The Devil blast you to hell and back you . . .

ANNA. Antosha! Language!

MAYOR (*vexed*). I can't worry about words now! (*To the*
SHOPKEEPERS.)] Did you know that Government Inspec-
tor you complained to is going to marry my daughter? Eh?
Did you know that? What do you say to that? [By God,
I'll show you, you're all swindlers, every one of you.
(*He singles out* ABDULLIN.) You, you're a swindler.
You make a hundred thousand on a Government contract
by supplying shoddy material, then offer twenty yards

of the same rubbish stuff to me and expect to get a medal for it! One word from me and you'd be – ah! Look at you, strutting about like turkey-cocks, thinking you're somebody! 'We're shopkeepers, we are, nobody can touch us, we're good as gentry any time, we are!' As if the gentry would . . . Ah! Pig-faces, what d'you know about gentry? At least they've got some manners, they got their hides tanned at school to some purpose, they know what's what. But you! You start off as swindlers and your masters beat you to teach you to swindle better! You learn how to give short measure before you've even learned the Lord's Prayer, and soon as your belly's fat enough and pockets full enough you start putting on airs! As if you were of the slightest significance to anyone! Just because you can empty a dozen samovars a day you think you're God's gift to Russia! Well, you're not. I don't give a damn for the whole pack of you!]

SHOPKEEPERS (*in chorus*). We're very sorry, Anton Antonovich!

MAYOR. You want to complain, do you? (*Singling out* ABDULLIN.) Who was it let you charge twenty thousand for timber for building the bridge, when the stuff you supplied wasn't worth a hundred? Eh? Wasn't it me? Wasn't it? You nanny-goat, you! I suppose you'd forgotten that? I've only got to whisper and the whole lot of you'll be off to Siberia! [What about that, then, eh?]

ABDULLIN. Before God, Anton Antonovich, we're all very sorry! The Devil must have tempted us, your Honour. [We'll never do anything like that again, as God's our witness!] Ask for anything you like, anything . . . but please don't be angry with us!

MAYOR. [Don't be angry with you! Look at you crawling at my feet! And for why? Because I'm on top, that's why. And if things had happened to go the other way you'd be trampling me in the mud, you pigs, and throwing logs on top just to make sure! I know you!

SHOPKEEPERS (*bowing again*). Don't ruin us, Anton Antonovich!]

MAYOR. Yes, it's 'Don't be angry with us' now, isn't it? But before, what was it before? (*He makes a menacing gesture.*) I'd like to . . . (*He stops, and shrugs.*) Well, I hope God forgives you, that's all. Lucky for you I'm not a vindictive man – but just you watch it from now on! My daughter isn't marrying some country yokel, remember – make sure your congratulations are appropriate – d'you understand? You'll not get away with a couple of salt cod and a barrel of sugarlumps this time! [Now go on, off with the lot of you!]

> *The* MAYOR *points to the door and the* SHOPKEEPERS *scurry out. Enter the* JUDGE *and the* CHARITY COMMISSIONER.

JUDGE. Anton Antonovich, my dear friend, is it really true? What a stroke of luck, eh?

CHARITY COMMISSIONER. Sincerest congratulations! I was delighted to hear of it, delighted! (*He crosses and kisses* ANNA'S *hand.*) Anna Andreyevna! (*He crosses to kiss* MARIA'S *hand.*) Maria Antonovna! Really delighted!

> *Enter* RASTAKOVSKY.

RASTAKOVSKY. Anton Antonovich! Congratulations! May God give you long life, and the happy couple too! And crowds of grandchildren and great-grandchildren! Anna Andreyevna! (*He kisses her hand.*) Maria Antonovna! (*He kisses her hand.*)

> *Enter* KOROBKIN *and* KOROBKIN'S *wife.*

KOROBKIN. I must congratulate you, Anton Antonovich, I must! Anna Andreyevna. (*He kisses her hand.*) Maria Antonovna! (*He kisses her hand.*)

KOROBKIN'S WIFE (*slyly*). Most *sincere* congratulations, Anna Andreyevna, on your *marvellous* good fortune!

LYULYUKOV (*entering*). A thousand congratulations, Anna Andreyevna! (*He kisses her hand; turns and clicks his heels.*) Maria Antonovna, a thousand congratulations.

> *He is followed by hordes of guests, all offering congratulations and kissing hands.* BOBCHINSKY *and* DOBCHINSKY *dash in, and push to the front.*

BOBCHINSKY. Allow me to congratulate you, Anton Antonovich!

DOBCHINSKY. Anton Antonovich, allow me to congratulate you on your good fortune!

BOBCHINSKY . . . on your good fortune!

DOBCHINSKY. Anna Andreyevna!

BOBCHINSKY. Anna Andreyevna!

They both try to kiss her hand at the same moment and knock their silly heads together.

DOBCHINSKY. Maria Antonovna! (*He kisses her hand.*) Allow me to congratulate you! I'm sure you'll be ever so happy, you'll wear dresses of gold and silver and drink the most wonderful soup [and live in a dream of pleasure!]

BOBCHINSKY (*interrupting*). Allow me, Maria Antonovna (*He kisses her hand.*) to congratulate you! I wish you all the wealth and happiness in the world – and a darling baby boy no bigger than this – (*He indicates the size.*) that you can hold in the palm of your hand! And what a noise the little rascal will make! (*He imitates a baby crying.*) Wah! Wah! Wah!

More GUESTS, *congratulations, kissing, the* SCHOOLS SUPERINTENDENT *and the* SCHOOLS SUPERINTENDENT'S WIFE *push through to the front.*

SCHOOLS SUPERINTENDENT. Allow me to congrat . . .

SCHOOLS SUPERINTENDENT'S WIFE (*running forward*). Ah, Anna Andreyevna, many congratulations, my dear! (*They kiss.*) I'm so happy and excited! 'Anna Andreyevna's daughter,' they told me, 'is going to marry that Government Inspector!' 'Heavens above,' I thought to myself. – and I was so pleased I ran straight to my husband. 'Luka,' I said, 'have you heard how lucky Anna Andreyevna's been?' So I told him. 'Thank God for that!' I thought to myself. And I said to Luka, 'Luka,' I said, 'I'm so happy, I can't wait to tell Anna Andreyevna how happy I am, she's always hoped for a good match for Maria, but *this* . . . she could hardly have dreamed.' Well, I was so happy I just cried, I couldn't say a word and Luka said, 'What on earth are you crying about?' and I said, 'Well, dear,' I said, 'I really don't know,' I said, and the tears just kept on coming and coming in torrents and Luka said . . .

MAYOR. Will you please all take a seat, Ladies and Gentlemen. (*Calling.*) Mishka! Bring some more chairs!

The GUESTS *seat themselves where they can.* MISHKA *brings chairs. Enter the* POLICE INSPECTOR *and a* CONSTABLE.

POLICE INSPECTOR. Allow me to congratulate Your Honour and wish you all prosperity and a long life!

MAYOR. Thank you, thank you. Do sit down, please.

JUDGE. Aren't you going to tell us how it all happened, Anton Antonovich, right from the beginning?

MAYOR. Well, it was a very funny business. His Excellency actually did the proposing himself . . .

ANNA (*taking it off him*). . . . in such a charming way, so gentle and considerate he was! Oh it was really lovely, the way he spoke! ['Anna Andreyevna,' he said, 'it's all due to your own exquisite virtues,' he said – oh it's lovely to have dealings with a real gentleman like that!] 'Believe me, Anna Andreyevna,' he said, 'my own life means nothing to me,' he said, 'I'm doing this purely out of regard for your own amazing qualities . . .'

MARIA. Oh Mamma, it was me he said that to!

ANNA. [Hold your tongue, girl, you know nothing about it, can't you learn not to interfere?] 'Anna Andreyevna,' he said to me, 'you're an astonishing woman,' he said. Oh, he said such lovely flattering things I can't tell you! [And then when I said we couldn't really hope for such an honour,] he fell right down on his knees in front of me [– really it was touching to see him!] And he said, 'Anna Andreyevna, [please don't make me unhappy,] say you respond to my feelings or I shall kill myself!'

MARIA. But really, Mamma, he was saying that about *me*!

ANNA. Well, I suppose it was about you as well, I never said it wasn't.

MAYOR. He quite frightened us, you know. 'My blood will be on your hands,' he kept saying.

ALL. No!
     Never!

Fancy that!

He never did!

SCHOOLS SUPERINTENDENT. It's the hand of destiny.

CHARITY COMMISSIONER. [Rubbish, destiny hasn't got any hands.] Nonsense. It's the just reward of true merit, that's what it is. (*Aside.*) The dirtiest pigs always root up the biggest acorns.

JUDGE. Anton Antonovich, you can have that puppy, you know, if you really want it.

MAYOR. I can't be bothered with puppies now.

JUDGE. You can have any one you like – take your pick!

KOROBKIN'S WIFE. [*Dearest* Anna Andreyevna,] I'm so *pleased* at your wonderful *luck*!

KOROBKIN. But where's the distinguished guest, then? Didn't someone tell me he'd left town?

MAYOR. Yes, he's gone off for a day or two on important business—

ANNA. —to visit his rich uncle and ask his blessing.

MAYOR. —ask his blessing, but he'll be back tomorrow or the – Assssssssssstishoooo! (*He sneezes – there is a general chorus of 'Bless you'!*) Thank you – tomorrow or the – AAAAAAA-TISHOOOOO! (*General blessings, some of them very loud.*) Thank you.

POLICE INSPECTOR. Good health to Your Honour!

BOBCHINSKY. May you live a hundred years and have a sack full of gold!

DOBCHINSKY. May you live over a hundred years and have several sacks of gold!

JUDGE (*aside*). Hope you die of the plague!

DOBCHINSKY'S WIFE (*aside*). May you burn in hell!

MAYOR. Thank you, thank you! And I wish you all the same!

ANNA. Of course, we shall be living in Petersburg, now. I'm afraid I find it awfully – provincial, here – not at all congenial. And my husband, of course (*She shrugs.*) will become a General.

MAYOR. I don't mind admitting I rather fancy being a General!

SCHOOLS SUPERINTENDENT. God grant you become one then!

RASTAKOVSKY (*aside*). To God, anything is possible!

JUDGE. Big ships must sail in deep waters!

CHARITY COMMISSIONER. And honours fall to the honourable!

JUDGE (*aside*). If they make him a general, it'll be like putting a saddle on a cow. [Still, he's not there yet, thank God. There's better men than him that aren't generals yet.]

CHARITY COMMISSIONER (*aside*). You never know; he might make it. He's conceited enough for it already. (*To the* MAYOR). You won't forget us, though, will you, Anton Antonovich?

JUDGE. If anything happened to go wrong here – you know, trouble – you'd help us, wouldn't you?

KOROBKIN. My son goes to Petersburg next year, to enter the service. I hope you'll keep an eye on the poor lad?

MAYOR. Of course, of course, I'll do everything I can, you know me.

ANNA. You're always much too ready to make promises, Antosha. You're not going to have time for little things like that. Anyway, why should you?

MAYOR. Why not, my dear? There's always time for helping a friend.

ANNA. I daresay, but you needn't go around promising to help every fool in the place.

KOROBKIN'S WIFE (*aside to the* SCHOOLS SUPERINTENDENT'S WIFE). Did you hear that? That's what she thinks of us!

SCHOOLS SUPERINTENDENT'S WIFE (*aside*). She's always been like that, the stupid bitch. No tact. Spit in her eye and she'll say it's the dew from heaven.

Enter the POSTMASTER, *waving a letter.*

POSTMASTER. Listen, all of you, listen, I've got some terrible news. The man we took for a Government Inspector wasn't the Inspector at all!

ALL. What!

Not the Inspector!

Not the Government Inspector!

POSTMASTER. Not the Government Inspector at all! It's all in this letter!

MAYOR. What letter?

POSTMASTER. This letter! One he wrote himself. It was brought down to my office, and I saw it was addressed to someone in Post Office Street, Petersburg, so of course I thought, 'Dear God, he's sending in a report about me.' So of course I opened it, to see.

MAYOR. How could you do such a thing!

POSTMASTER. I don't know myself, I really don't – there seemed to be a supernatural force egging me on. [I was just going to send it off, express, when suddenly I was seized by a curiosity stronger than anything I'd ever known before. I felt I couldn't do it, I couldn't open it, but all the time something was compelling me to break the seal! In one ear there was a voice whispering, 'Don't touch that seal, you'll be in trouble if you do,' but then in the other ear another voice, even stronger, was saying, 'Go on, break the seal, open it up!' And soon as I touch that wax, seemed my blood was afire, and when I open up the letter, I was all ice, trembling all over and nearly fainting!]

MAYOR. How dare you open a letter from such an important personage!

POSTMASTER. Aha, that's just it, Anton Antonovich, he's not important at all! He isn't a personage, either!

MAYOR. What is he, then?

POSTMASTER. He's nothing, a nobody! I don't know what you could call him.

MAYOR (angrily). [What the devil do you mean?] How dare you call him a nobody! I'll have you arrested!

POSTMASTER. Who? You?

MAYOR. Yes. Me!

POSTMASTER. You wouldn't do that.

MAYOR. Wouldn't I? Do you realise he's going to marry my daughter? I'll be a personage myself then, and I'll have you packed off to Siberia if you don't watch it.

POSTMASTER. You don't want to be talking about Siberia,

Anton Antonovich! Siberia's a long way off. I best read you the letter, I think, shall I read it out, then?

ALL. Yes, yes!

Read it!

Read us the letter!

POSTMASTER. Right, then. Hrchm. 'My dear Tryapichkin, Extraordinary things have been happening to me. On my way home I was completely cleaned out by a very sharp infantry officer, so there I was, holed up in the wretched little inn here and being threatened by the innkeeper because I couldn't pay my bill when suddenly – I suppose because of my Petersburg clothes and looks – I found the whole town had mistaken me for some Government Inspector, [and everything changed completely!] Here I am now, living a life of luxury in the Mayor's house, flirting with his wife and daughter both at the same time! I haven't made up my mind yet which I'll go for first – the wife's probably the best bet, she looks as if she's ready for anything! [Remember the days when we were so hard up we had to live on our wits, and the time that confectioner threw us out on our necks because I'd told him to "book those pies to the King of England's account"! It's a bit different here, I can tell you!] They're all falling over themselves to lend me money – as much as I ask for! Honestly, you'd die laughing, they're such nitwits! I know you write bits and pieces for the theatre sometimes – you really ought to put this lot in a play, it would be a riot! First there's the Mayor, you can see at a glance he's a crook – though not a very clever one . . .'

MAYOR. Rubbish! I don't believe that's there!

POSTMASTER (showing him the letter). See for yourself.

MAYOR (reading). '. . . crook . . . not a very clever . . .' You must have written that in yourself!

POSTMASTER. Don't be silly, how could I?

CHARITY COMMISSIONER. Oh, read on!

POSTMASTER (reading again). 'The Mayor . . . see at a glance he's a crook . . .'

MAYOR. Dammit, you don't have to keep repeating it! We've all heard that bit!

POSTMASTER. Mm . . . Mmmmmmm . . . a . . . not a very
clever one '. . . The Postmaster – er – the Postmaster's a
good enough fellow . . .' (*Pause.*) Well, there's something a
bit rude [about me] here, I'll go on to . . .

MAYOR. No, no, read it!

POSTMASTER. Why should I?

MAYOR. If you're supposed to be reading the letter, get on and
read it – all of it!

CHARITY COMMISSIONER. Here, let me read it. (*He takes the
letter, puts on his spectacles and reads.*) 'The Postmaster's a
half-blind half-wit, though he's sharp enough to tamper
with the mail when he feels like it . . .'

POSTMASTER (*to the listeners*). The young scamp! [He ought to
be whipped!]

CHARITY COMMISSIONER. Hm! (*Reading.*) 'Then there's the
Charity Comm – Comm – Comm—' (*He stops.*)

KOROBKIN. What's stopping you now?

CHARITY COMMISSIONER. It's – er – a bit difficult to read.
You can see he's a proper rascal, though.

KOROBKIN (*trying to take the letter*). Give it here, my eyes are
better than yours.

CHARITY COMMISSIONER. No, it's all right. I'll read it. It's
legible enough further on.

POSTMASTER. No, let's hear it all, we've had it all so far!

ALL. Give it to him!

Let him have it!

Let Korobkin read it!

CHARITY COMMISSIONER. Oh, all right, [here you are.
There, look, you begin there.] (*He covers part of the letter
with his fingers.*)

They all crowd round, exclaiming.

POSTMASTER. No, come on, now, read the whole thing!

KOROBKIN (*removing the* CHARITY COMMISSIONER'S *hand*).
'The Charity Commissioner, Zemlyanika, looks just like –'
it's quite easy to read – 'just like a pig in a wig . . .'

CHARITY COMMISSIONER. Really! It's not even funny!
Whoever heard of a pig in a wig! (*He shrugs.*)

KOROBKIN (*reading*). 'The Schools Superintendent can't

speak for twitching – he's frightened of his own shadow . . .'

SCHOOLS SUPERINTENDENT. What does he mean, t-t-twitch-t-twitching . . . ?

JUDGE (*aside*). Nothing about me so far, thank God!

KOROBKIN (*reading*). 'The Judge . . .'

JUDGE. Look here, this letter's far too long, it's getting boring, [What's the point in listening to all this rubbish?]

SCHOOLS SUPERINTENDENT. Oh, no, you don't!

POSTMASTER. Go on reading. We might as well hear it all, now.

KOROBKIN (*reading*). 'The Judge, Lyapkin-Tyapkin, thinks so much about his dogs that he's beginning to look like one!'

JUDGE. Well, there's nothing wrong in looking like a dog! Some dogs are very beautiful!

KOROBKIN (*reading*). ['On the whole, though, they're quite a friendly, good-hearted bunch.] I'll say goodbye now, old chap. I've decided to follow your example and devote myself to literature, my life's getting to be an awful bore and one really ought to do something about nourishing the intellect. [I'm beginning to feel I ought to devote myself to some of the higher things of life.] Write to me [at Podkatilovka] in Saratov. Your old friend, Ivan Alexandrovich Khlyestakov.' [(*He turns over the letter and reads the address.*) It's addressed to: Ivan Vassilyevich, Ninety-seven, first on the right through the courtyard, third floor, Post Office Street, Saint Petersburg.]

KOROBKIN'S WIFE. Oh, but it's all so dreadful!

MAYOR. This is going to kill me. I'm starting to die already. Oh, my eyes, my eyes, something's happening to my eyes. . . . All I can see are pigs' snouts, pigs' snouts everywhere! Where is he? Bring him back! Bring him back!

POSTMASTER. How can we bring him back? I told them to give him the fastest horses we've got [and God knows why but I gave him a note to the other posting stations to give him their best horses too!

KOROBKIN'S WIFE. What a mess it all is.] I've never known anything like it!

JUDGE (*wailing*). But I lent him three hundred roubles!

POSTMASTER. So did I!

SCHOOLS SUPERINTENDENT. So did I!

CHARITY COMMISSIONER. I lent him four hundred!

BOBCHINSKY. And Peter Ivanovich and I lent him sixty-five between us!

JUDGE (*spreading his hands*). But how did it happen!? That's what I want to know! How could we make such a stupid mistake?

MAYOR (*striking his forehead*). Oh, God, how could I be such a fool. I must be losing my wits in my old age! Thirty years I've been in public service, and no one's ever got the better of me! I've beaten the worst swindlers [in the country] at their own game. I've cheated cheats who could have cheated the whole human race out of immortality! I've bamboozled three Governors in a row ... (*He waves his hand dismissively.*) [... as if Governors were anything to worry about ...]

ANNA. But it's impossible, Antosha! [After all,] he's engaged to Maria!

MARIA *weeps.*

MAYOR (*furious*). Engaged! [Bah! Don't you give me your 'engaged'!] (*In a frenzy.*) Look at me – come on – look! Every Christian and heathen and savage in the world – come and have a look at the Mayor, look at the fool he's made of himself! Fool! (*He shakes his fist at himself.*) Taking that jumped-up little worm, [that bag of rubbish,] for a personage! Think of him bowling along now, with all his bells a-jingle, laughing his blasted head off! He'll tell his dirty little tale all over Russia. I shall be a laughing-stock. Some inky little scribbler'll put us all in a play, yes, every one of you! That'll hurt, I promise you! He won't spare us – rank, position, appearance, anything to make an audience snigger, it'll all go in! (*He suddenly turns on the audience.*) What do you think you're laughing at, eh?! You're laughing at yourselves, do you know that? Ah, what's the use? (*Sudden access of fury; he dances with rage.*) I'd like to get my hands on all those writers, damned snivelling liberals, the lot of you! I'd grind you into a jelly and kick you to hell and gone, you filthy parasites! (*He grinds all writers under his heel.*)

Pause.

[I'm not thinking straight. Those whom the Gods wish to punish, they first drive mad. Very true in my case!] (*Pause.*) What was there about that little tick that made us take him for a Government Inspector? Eh? What was there? Not that much! (*He measures off the tip of his finger.*) But there you all were, buzzing around, crying 'The Inspector, it's the Inspector, it must be the Inspector.' Well? Whose idea was it first, eh? Tell me that! (*He glares round.*)

CHARITY COMMISSIONER. For the life of me, I can't remember. [I can't seem to think straight, either.]

JUDGE. I'll tell you who started it! It was those two! (*He points to* BOBCHINSKY *and* DOBCHINSKY.)

BOBCHINSKY. It wasn't me! It never crossed my mind!

DOBCHINSKY. I didn't have anything to do with it!

CHARITY COMMISSIONER. Yes, it was! Of course it was those two!

SCHOOLS SUPERINTENDENT. That's right, they came scampering in here straight from the Inn like a pair of lunatics. 'He's here, he's here already! He won't part with any money! It must be him!' A fine bird you chose, the two of you!

MAYOR. Oh, yes, you nosy parkers, it would be you, wouldn't it? The town gossips!

CHARITY COMMISSIONER. To hell with them!

MAYOR. [All you two blockheads can do is snoop around town getting everyone into a tangle with your daft tales! You're a fine pair of boobies, aren't you.]

JUDGE. Bunglers!

SCHOOLS SUPERINTENDENT. Thick-heads!

CHARITY COMMISSIONER. Pot-bellied pair of idiots!

Everyone crowds round, accusing them.

BOBCHINSKY. It wasn't me, really it wasn't. It was Peter Ivanovich, who first . . .

DOBCHINSKY. No, no, Peter Ivanovich, it was you who said it first . . .

BOBCHINSKY. It wasn't me, you were the first, you were the first . . .

Enter a GENDARME *in splendid uniform.*

GENDARME (*announces superbly*). The Government Inspector from Saint Petersburg has arrived, with instructions from the Tsar. He demands your immediate attendance at the Inn.

Tableau of consternation.

CURTAIN

Notes

The following Notes are indebted to editions of the play in Russian edited by M. Beresford (1996) and by W. Harrison (1964).

p.2 *Don't blame the mirror if your face is lopsided*: or 'Don't blame the mirror if your mug (*rozha*) is crooked'. Gogol added this proverb as epigraph to the 1842 edition of the play.

5 *begun at the bottom*: 's nizkikh chinov' (from the lowest ranks). The reference here is to the infamous 'Table of Ranks' instituted by Peter the Great with which Russian officialdom became obsessed. There were fourteen grades and most civilian ranks had a military, naval and courtly equivalent. At the top was Imperial Chancellor/Commander-in-Chief, and at the bottom Collegiate Registrar, which was so low it had no equivalent in other areas. Chichikov in *Dead Souls* is a Grade 6 Collegiate Councillor/Colonel and 'The Nose' in that bizarre fiction is a Grade 5 State Councillor/Brigadier. Each grade had its own mode of address. 'Your Supreme Excellency' related to Grades 1 and 2, 'Your High Excellency' to Grades 3 and 4, 'Your Excellency' to Grade 5, 'Your Supreme Honour' to Grades 6–8 and 'Your Honour' to Grades 9–14. These ranks were worked out on Danish and Prussian models and meant little to the vast bulk of the Russian population. Khlyestakov is at the bottom of the pile.
of which the most striking features are the buttons and button-holes: 's petlitsami' means simply 'with button loops' rather than holes, the loops being elaborately

woven and attached to the left-hand side of the frock-coat, looping over the buttons on the right.

not exactly old yet: Anna Andreyevna claimed to be thirty-two in an earlier version of the play but is probably nearer forty.

anthology verse: the most popular and easy to read.

'not quite all there': the Russian expression 'bez tsaria v golove' suggests 'muddle-headed' or 'without a single fixed idea in his head'.

6   *dresses very fashionably*: he would probably wear a black or dark blue tail-coat, plain or striped trousers of a different colour, a waistcoat, a shirt with frilly front and cuffs, a cravat, white gloves, patent leather shoes and a top hat.

8   The accents above each first name, patronymic and surname in the cast list indicate where the stress falls in pronunciation.

UKHOVYORTOV: a name based on the words 'ukho' (ear) and 'vertet' (to twist or turn). So something like 'Inspector Ear-yanker'.

9   *THE SERGEANT'S WIDOW*: only the Mayor claims that she is 'a widow', when exonerating himself from having her flogged. Despite the fact that her husband has been called up for military service, there is no indication that he is dead and she is referred to in the original cast list, and in the scene in which she appears, as 'wife'.

ABDULLIN: the name indicates Muslim Asian origin.

MISHKA: diminutive of Misha which is the colloquial abbreviation of Mikhail (Michael), hence 'Mick'. As a young serving lad he would wear the cossack dress which was usual for serfs who served the gentry.

A GENDARME: the one character in the play who, significantly or otherwise, is missing from Gogol's original cast list.

LYULYUKOV: from 'lyulyukat' (to rock a cradle).

RASTAKOVSKY: a retired military officer who, in the first version of the play, has a separate scene with the doctor.

His name would seem to derive from 'rastakat'sia' 'to agree in servile fashion', in other words he is 'a creep'.

KOROBKIN: the name derives from 'korobka' (a box). He and the last two characters referred to above are described by Gogol in the cast list as 'distinguished persons of the town'.

SVISTUNOV: from 'svistun' (whistler).

PUGOVITZIN: from 'pugovitsa', meaning 'a button'. 'Pugat' also means 'to frighten'.

DYERZHIMORDA: from 'derzhat' (to hold) and 'morda' (gob), so 'PC Shutyergob'.

Townspeople: Gogol is specific and refers to 'meshchane' (the lower citizenry) who, according to a charter of 1785, were so classified because they possessed less than 1,000 roubles; and 'kuptsy' (merchants), here rendered as 'shopkeepers'.

Act One, Scene One

All are in civilian dress during this act except the Mayor and Postmaster who wear uniform. In the original, the Police Inspector (or Superintendent) is also present although Gogol, later, appears to lose sight of the fact.

11   *Government Inspector*: a 'revizor' in Russian who, in the reign of Nicholas I, frequently travelled as a private individual. It was Peter the Great who 'introduced financial inspectors to uncover financial abuses and also appoint a chief inspector to report to the Senate. Under Nicholas I administrative inspections were generally carried out by a high-ranking officer, sometimes by a senior official or a senator. Such visitations, which often lasted for several months, were made on an *ad hoc* basis, usually after the authorities in St Petersburg had been apprised of irregularities in one of the provinces. The inspectors took so long to reach their destination that, despite the secrecy surrounding their activities, the local officials nearly always had prior warning of their arrival

and were able to arrange a cover-up' (Gogol, 1996, pp.190–1).

Petersburg: the imperial capital of Russia, built by decree of Peter the Great during the early eighteenth century in the Italian renaissance style and situated on the Baltic Sea. Gogol's *Petersburg Tales* evince his fascination with the city as well as his mixed feelings about its bureaucratic and cultural atmosphere. The city was named after Saint Peter (rather than the Tsar) and was rechristened Petrograd during the First World War, then Leningrad in honour of the Bolshevik leader following his death in 1924, before reverting to its original name following the collapse of the Soviet Union in the early 1990s.

incognito: from Latin 'incognitus' meaning 'unknown'. According to the OED the term means 'concealed under a disguised or assumed character'.

Chmikhov: he is 'Andrei Ivanovich Chmikhov' in the original, which is important for establishing his relationship with the other people described in the letter (see following note on patronymics and note to p.12).

Artemy Philipovich: all Russians are given a first name and a patronymic, the latter being the name of their father – so, in this case, Artemy is the son of Philip. By the same token, the Mayor was named after his own father, Anton son of Anton, while his wife Anna's patronymic tells us that her father was called Andrei.

five hundred roubles: the rouble is the standard unit of currency in Russia. There are a hundred kopeks in a rouble.

12   *the perquisites of your office*: a euphemistic way of referring to the bribes which the Mayor is in the habit of accepting, bribery being an important theme of the play and a comment on a commonly accepted corrupt practice in Gogol's Russia.

My sister Anna Kirilovna and her husband . . . Ivan Kirilovich has put on a lot of weight: it looks as if Anna Kirilovna is married to Ivan Kirilovich, but if Anna is the letter writer's (Andrei Ivanovich's) sister, they do not have the same patronymic. In fact, Anna must be the letter writer's cousin and Ivan Kirilovich must be her brother, as they share the same patronymic.

13   *a civilised man can't breathe in the place*: in the original, 'the sick smoke such strong tobacco that you have a sneezing fit whenever you go in there'. Sneezing may be said to play a symbolic role in the play, associated with the presence of malevolent forces, which is why we say, superstitiously, 'Bless you'. It also helps to explain why the Mayor has a sneezing fit towards the end of the play.

DISTRICT PHYSICIAN *(beaming)*. *Ja. Onderstand everyt'ing!*: Gogol simply puts a stage direction at this point: '*(Christian Ivanovich emits a sound mid-way between "ee" and "eh")*'.

he stinks of vodka: vodka is strong drink, similar to gin but distilled from rye, which is widely drunk in Russia and which like gin is colourless but, as implied here, not odourless.

14   DISTRICT PHYSICIAN: *Ja, garlick. Gut! (He beams.)*: 'Yes, garlic. Good!' Gogol repeats the stage direction '*(Christian Ivanovich emits the same sound as before)*'.

Voltaire can say what he likes: the famous French rationalist philosopher Voltaire (1694–1778).

What's more, Anton: the Judge's name is 'Amos'.

15   *Prince Miloffsky*: 'our Marshal of the Nobility', in the original and no specific name is mentioned. A Marshal of the Nobility was 'a powerful figure in the locality, head of the landowning gentry in the district or province, elected to preside over their triennial assembly and represent their interests in organs of local government' (Gogol, 1996, p.199).

the Assyrians and the Babylonians: the Assyrians were the inhabitants of an empire in the Middle East, *c*.2500–612 BC, in northern Mesopotamia (now Iraq), whose capital was Ninevah. At its greatest extent, the empire included Egypt and extended as far as the Persian Gulf. The Babylonians were the inhabitants of ancient Babylonia situated on the left bank of the River Euphrates (also now part of modern Iraq).

Alexander the Great: 356–323 BC, king of Macedonia, an ancient country of south-east Europe between Illyria, Thrace and the Aegean Sea, and conqueror of the Persian Empire. He also founded Alexandria in what is present-day Egypt, which became the centre of Hellenistic civilisation.

Enter the Postmaster: 'The Postmaster, being on duty, wears his uniform, which is green, like that of the Governor, but with a stand-up collar of black velvet and matching cuffs decorated with lace. His trousers and waistcoat are pale yellow' (Gogol, 1996, p.201).

16   *There's going to be war with the Turks*: Russia had waged a successful war against Turkey in 1828–9. In the long conflict between the two countries, France supported the Turks and, together with Britain, considered the growth of Russian influence to be a danger. The so-called 'Eastern Question' later led to the Crimean War.

no denunciation or anything: according to Beresford, 'Informing had been officially encouraged in Russia since the Code of 1649 made denunciation of plotters against the crown mandatory under pain of death. Successive tsarist governments came to rely on private citizens for information about seditious or illegal activities. Under Nicholas I the Third Section had many informers on its pay-roll' (Gogol, 1996, p.202). The same could be said of Stalinist Russia where the equivalent of the Third Section (the secret police) was the KGB.

Some people's letters are so interesting: the interception and inspection of private correspondence is something we associate more with Soviet Russia, but it was common practice in nineteenth-century Russia as well.

17   *Saratov and Kostroma*: important trading centres. Kostroma is situated to the north-east of Moscow; Saratov is on the lower Volga.

'My life is spent in the Elysian fields': the place which, in

Greek mythology, the souls of the blessed inhabit after death.

Moscow on fire: the reference to Moscow being set on fire harks back to the Napoleonic invasion of 1812 when Muscovites resorted to setting fire to their own city in order to frustrate Napoleon's attempts to capture it.

Tcheptovich is suing Varhovinsky . . . on both their estates: the Judge, who should be impartial, is openly admitting that, unknown to each litigant, he is taking bribes from both and playing one off against the other while enjoying the rights both afford him to go shooting on their respective estates.

18   *As soon as I had the pleasure . . . after you'd had that upsetting letter*: an important piece of exposition. Although the scene is not shown, before the play proper begins we are to understand that Bobchinsky has been informed by the Mayor of the contents of Chmikhov's letter before anyone else in the town has been told, otherwise there is no reason for him and Dobchinsky to identify the person at the inn as the Government Inspector.

19   *Pochechuev*: the name derives from the popular word for haemorrhoids, 'piles'.

I've had nothing to eat all day: food and its consumption is a significant theme in the play. It has been examined by, among others, Jan Kott in his 'The Eating of the Government Inspector' in *Theatre Quarterly*, March–May 1975, reprinted in his book *Theatre of Essence*, Evanston, Illinois, 1985.

As if he'd got a lot . . . up here: Bobchinsky is suggesting that Khlyestakov is very intelligent, whereas Gogol makes the point that he is fairly brainless.

20   *you've got a lithp*: in Russian this is not the same as the tendency in English to say 'th' instead of 's' but to pronounce 's' as 'sh' and 'z' as 'zh' (the 'zh' sound as in 'pleasure').

everything on credit: there were no credit cards in nineteenth-century Russia so what one owed was simply recorded unofficially 'on tick' until such time as the person could, or was forced to, pay the bill, when no more 'credit' was forthcoming.

21   *St Basil's Day*: 'the feast day of St Basil the Egyptian' in the original, which does not appear in the calendar of the Russian Orthodox Church. The best known St Basil is the one after whom the onion-domed church on Red Square is named.

A good reputation stands still, it's the bad ones that run like the wind: the play is full of pithy colloquialisms, such as this one implying that scandalous behaviour is spread abroad by gossip far more readily than good behaviour. The translators have substituted this expression for the original's rather more obscure: 'That's how it's set down in *The Deeds of John Mason*'.

It's a stupid mouse that only knows one hole: the implication here is that one needs to know more than one way out of a difficult situation.

a chink in their armour: a point where they are vulnerable (in this case on account of inexperience or immaturity).

You've all got muck in your own backyards: the kind of vulgar colloquialism which offended audiences when the play was first staged. The Mayor is implying that everyone has something to hide from a Government Inspector so had better set about concealing it.

Run and fetch the Superintendent: Gogol may have forgotten that the Superintendent has been on stage all along according to his stage directions in the original at the beginning of the act.

22   *beef tea*: beef tea or beef extract was thought to be nourishing and easily digested, and was given to invalids.

cabbage soup: 'shchi', in Russian, a cheap and basic peasant dish.

Solomon: Israelite king of the tenth century BC noted for his judgement.

The JUDGE . . . go out: Gogol omits to mention the departure of the doctor with everyone else.

23   *in the carriage*: a 'droshki', which only carried two passengers. It was an open carriage and therefore only used during the summer months.

   I'll run along behind: Bobchinsky makes a verbal slip here. He says he will follow along behind 'petukhom' (like a cockerel) when he means to say 'peshkom' (on foot). This prepares the audience for the Mayor's verbal slip when he confuses a street with a broom, although the two expressions 'po ulitse' (a street each) and 'po metle' (a broom each) are less similar.

   broadcloth: 'fine, plain-weave, dressed, double-width, black cloth, used chiefly for men's garments. (The term now implies quality rather than width)' OED.

   you're taking more than you're entitled to: one of the most famous lines in the play which, in the original, reads: 'ne po chinu beresh!' (You take more than your position [in the Table of Ranks] entitles you to!).

24   *to see if the fire-engine's working*: the police also operated the fire-engines in nineteenth-century Russia.

   I'll light Him the biggest candle He's ever seen!: special candles are bought and lit in the Russian Orthodox Church when making a request or thanking patron saints, the Virgin or the Almighty for help. In fact, the Mayor intends lighting a candle to his own patron saint, Antony, not to God Himself.

   (He picks up the hatbox): it is important that the confusion between hatbox and hat be a genuine one so it has to be a specially designed hatbox shaped to look like the cocked hat which it contains. This mistaking of one thing for another follows the Mayor's verbal confusion between 'broom' and 'street'. The ultimate confusion is his mistaking a humble clerk for a Government Inspector.

25   *walking about in nothing but their shirts*: 'To keep cool while working in hot weather Russian peasants often wore a knee-length shirt and boots, but not trousers. Soldiers followed the same practice, but were required to wear full uniform when appearing in public. This

reference to the soldiers going about trouserless makes clear, incidentally, that the play is set in late spring or summer' (Gogol, 1996, p.216).

Antosha: affectionate diminutive form of 'Anton'.

26   *what sort of moustache he's got*: the Mayor's wife wants to know whether he is 'moustachioed', which suggests that she wants to know whether he is a military person or not since army officers, after 1837, were required to wear moustaches (which extended from the upper lip to the cheeks) while civilian officials were required to be clean-shaven (Gogol, 1996, p.216).

Act One, Scene Two (Act Two, Scene One in the original)

27   *a bit of the ready*: ready money, i.e. money to hand.

      on the ferry: St Petersburg is built both on the mainland and on a number of islands with the River Neva flowing between. The only way across the river, or between islands, prior to the building of the first permanent bridge in 1850, was by ferry.

      there's a back door to every house: most of the dwellings in the city are blocks of flats built around a central courtyard into which a main entrance leads. Having been driven into one courtyard it is possible to escape on foot into an adjoining courtyard and avoid paying the fare.

      finest English cloth: English cloth had a universal reputation for quality during the nineteenth century.

28   *the Nevsky*: Nevsky Prospect, St Petersburg's main thoroughfare.

      the old master: Khlyestakov's father. They are travelling from St Petersburg in answer to a paternal summons from Khlyestakov's father to answer for his son's apparent lack of success on the promotional ladder.

      Gawd, I'm so hungry I could eat a salt mine: Russia, and especially Siberia, is noted for its salt mines to which convicts were sent for punishment with hard labour.

29   *Penza*: a provincial capital some 380 miles south-east of

Moscow on the River Sura, a tributary of the Volga.

Had this amazing gift for dealing himself the ace!: in other words, he was a skilful cheat. In the original, Khlyestakov states that the infantry officer cut the cards amazingly well at *stoss*, which is a card game and a variant of faro, in which the players bet on the order in which certain cards will appear when taken singly from the top of the pack.

31 *Mademoiselle, enchanté*: 'Mademoiselle, [I am] delighted/ charmed [to meet you].'

Mais vous sommes si beaux: 'But you are so beautiful.' He should, in fact, say 'Vous êtes si belle', but employs the wrong tense and the wrong gender as well as the adjectival plural form instead of the singular.

34 *fish-glue*: Dutch or Flanders glue of a very fine texture.

my little children: the Mayor has only one, grown-up, child of course. He is behaving like a poverty-stricken mother in appealing for sympathy.

35 *That story . . . the Sergeant's widow flogged*: we later hear from the lady herself that he did have her flogged. She is, in fact, the Sergeant's wife (see note to p.9). The flogging of wives was forbidden by law but widows were seemingly exempt by legal default, hence the Mayor's lying reference to her widowhood just in case it is found out that he did have her beaten.

36–7 *They say travel broadens the mind . . . it isn't only the mind that gets broadened*: road travel in Russia to this day, especially in the countryside, is an extremely uncomfortable experience because of the poor state of the roads which, in many cases, are little more than dirt tracks.

37 *they bite like wolf-hounds*: Russian inns were noted for their uncleanliness and for the prevalence of bedbugs. There is a degree of alliteration in the original which suggests that 'bloodhounds' or 'borzois' could replace 'wolf-hounds'.

39 *that local Madeira*: Madeira is a wine like sherry that comes from Madeira and would not be easy to obtain in

the provinces. The Mayor drinks a local version which is probably much rougher.

Act One, Scene Three (Act Three, Scene One in the original)

41   *Mamma*: diminutives are always difficult to translate. *Maminka*, in the original, is more like 'mummy', or even 'mummikins'. 'Mamma' is the Russian for 'mum' and is pronounced as in 'marmite' with the stress on the first syllable.

43   *How long will they be . . . The sheer treachery of it!*: This section has been added by the translators to clarify the action.

44   *Now, Maria*: her mother calls her 'Mashenka', which is a further diminutive of 'Masha' in place of the more formal 'Maria'. Difficult to find an English equivalent. Stress on the first syllable with the 'a' pronounced as is 'car'.

45   *Oh, yes – he's very general*: 'Yes, he's a general, but in sort of reverse order', in the original. Ossip is implying that if the Table of Ranks was reversed then a Grade 14 clerk would be a Grade 2 General.

46   *(bobbing up beside KHLYESTAKOV)*: in an earlier version of the play Gogol had the corpulent Zemlyanika 'running forward as light on his feet as a twenty-two-year-old dandy'.
      recovering like flies: a humorous inversion of the more common 'dying like flies', an idiom which is the same in Russian as in English.

48   *if you make the mistake of backing out* [i.e. sticking, as in pontoon] *just when you ought to be doubling your stakes*: Beresford explains: 'In *faro*, *bank* or *stoss* . . . a punter would declare that he was sticking by saying *basta* (from Italian 'enough') . . . In these same games of chance the punter would bend over [first one] corner and then a second and a third corner of his winning card to indicate that he was doubling his stake plus gains . . . on the next turn, trying to end up with 4, 8 and 16 times his stake respectively . . . He could thus win up to four times in

succession with the same card if it made a double with
that placed to the left by the banker at each turn of two
cards' (Gogol, 1996, p.246).

tediosity: a pretentious, but non-existent word in English. The noun is 'tediousness'.

comprenny-vous: 'comprenez-vous' (You understand/
know). French was the language largely spoken by the
Russian aristocracy in preference to Russian.

49   *Ça, c'est la vivre!*: Khlyestakov's garbled French trans-
lates, literally, as 'That's the to live!'. What he should
say is, 'Ça, c'est la vie' (That's the life!).

copy-clerk: a clerical official whose sole (and soul-
destroying) task was to copy letters and other documents laboriously in longhand. This was before the days
of typewriters and carbon paper, or of photocopiers.

standing on ceremony: observing the finer points of
decorum which, in this case, involves not sitting down
in the presence of a high-ranking dignitary.

50   *'Well, Pushkin, old boy*: this reference to Russia's greatest
poet (1799–1837) with whom Gogol, rather than
Khlyestakov, was on friendly terms, comes from the
revised version of the play and was added after the
poet's tragic and untimely death in a duel.

Don Juan, Romeo and Juliet: Byron's poem (or Molière's
play) and the work of Shakespeare have been substituted here for the original's *Robert le Diable* (an opera by
Meyerbeer) and *Norma*, Bellini's opera of 1831. The
reference to *The Marriage of Figaro* may be to Beau-
marchais' play or to Mozart's opera based on it.

The Moscow Telegraph: a fortnightly journal published in
St Petersburg between 1825 and 1834 when it was
closed down by the authorities.

Baron Brambeus: pen-name of Osip Senkovsky, an
orientalist who edited what was, at the time, Russia's
most widely read periodical.

Youri Miloslavsky: a patriotic historical novel by Mikhail
Zagoskin who, as it happens, also directed the first
Moscow production of *The Government Inspector*.

51   *my little fourth-floor flat . . . I live on the first floor*:
Khlyestakov inadvertently confesses that he lives on the
less desirable, because cheaper, upper floor. The first
floor in Russia would normally be our ground floor but
here refers to the 'beletazh' which was the most
expensive and most desirable dwelling level between the
ground and first floor.

    thirty-five thousand messengers: Gogol increased the num-
ber of messengers with each revision of the play from
none to fifteen, to thirty-five thousand.

52   *the Privy Council*: the Council of State, instituted by
Aleksandr I in 1810 and 'the highest consultative body
of the Russian Empire' (Gogol, 1996, p.256).

    the Palace: the Winter Palace, a magnificent baroque
building on the banks of the Neva in Petersburg, now a
museum, as opposed to the Summer Palace (Petrodvor-
etz) just outside the city.

53   *Generalissimo*: a rare title conferred on generals who
commanded several armies, rather than just a single
one.

    We aren't even in proper uniform: all public officials were
required to wear uniform when on duty.

54   *if you drop a brick*: if you commit an indiscretion or make
a *faux pas*.

55   *(he pulls his forelock)*: a gesture of respect.

Act Two (Act Four, Scene One in the original)

58   *dress by the right*: a military command to indicate that
they are to stand in a straight line with each taking the
measure of distance from, and straightness with, the
person on their immediate right by raising the right arm
and shuffling into line with that person.

    (rubbing finger and thumb together): a gesture which hints
at the power of money (in this case of bribery).

59   *he's already broken bread with you*: a rather highfalutin,
even religiose, way of mentioning that Khlyestakov has
already dined with the Charity Commissioner at the

hospital. Zemlyanika is, of course, determined to go in last so as to denounce the others.

Cicero: writer and statesman of Ancient Rome noted for his oratorical powers.

60   *Elected in 1816 for a three-year term . . . held the post ever since*: no mention of re-election.

the St Anne: 'St Anne, Third Class', in the original, which was three degrees lower than the St Vladimir, Fourth Class. Both were awarded to civil servants.

61   *Civil Officer Sixth Class*: 'nadvornyi sovetnik', i.e. a court councillor of the seventh grade equivalent to lieutenant-colonel.

bon ton: French, meaning high society, the well-bred.

62   *Civil Off. Sec. Class*: 'titulyarnyi sovetnik', i.e. of the ninth civil service grade and equivalent to the rank of captain. He is the lowest grade town official.

64   *Civil Captain Third Class*: 'nadvornyi sovetnik'. Zemlyanika has, in fact, the same rank as the Postmaster.

65   *an anarchist*: someone who does not believe in observing the laws of civil society and who does not recognise any ruling authority. The reference at this point in the play is to 'a Jacobin'. The Jacobins were, in fact, dedicated to the maintenance and propagation of extreme democracy and absolute equality in the wake of the French Revolution of 1789, although the term became a byword in Russia for extreme radicals and freethinkers.

Perpetua: Latin 'perpetuo' meaning 'constantly', 'perpetually'. The name is 'Perpetuya' in the original and an unusual name for a child, but designed to suggest the unchanging nature of the offspring in the world of the play just as earlier the son of Vlass the innkeeper seems doomed to become another version of his father.

66   *State Bonds*: his money is tied up in government bonds, a system set up by Catherine the Great by which the state sold bonds to people who wanted to earn interest on their money in return for the state having the use of it for a period of time.

67   *But I want my son to have my name*: illegitimate sons

were barred from entering government service, hence Dobchinsky's otherwise bizarre-seeming request. Nicholas I, unlike tsars before him, 'had refused to legitimise children born out of wedlock' (Gogol, 1996, p.271).

68 *Tryapichkin*: with the stress on *ich*. A 'tryapka', with the stress on the *ya*, is 'a rag'. 'The name has become a byword for a gossip columnist' (Gogol, 1996, p.272).

69 *a silver rouble*: paper currency was constantly subject to devaluation but a silver rouble held its value because made of the real thing.

71 *We're generous enough to him on his name day*: a name day is not a birthday but the day of the saint after whom the person is named.

He'll billet a whole regiment on you: 'From the time of Peter the Great civilians were required by law to house and feed soldiers stationed in areas where there were no permanent barracks' (Gogol, 1996, p.275).

ought to be sent straight to Siberia!: not only the site of salt mines but of forced labour camps right through to the end of Soviet times.

73 *Poshlyopkin*: from the verb 'poshlyopat' (to slap or spank), with the stress on the *yo*.

And him a married man, that's against the law!: this was not true but the Mayor may have used his powers to influence the Recruitment Board who would not normally prioritise the recruitment of a married man before a bachelor or an older son before a younger.

three bolts of good linen: a bolt is a roll of woven fabric, usually of a definite length such as thirty yards.

74 *I couldn't sit down for two days*: in an earlier version of the play, the Sergeant's wife had offered to show Khlyestakov 'the marks' where she had been beaten but the Imperial censor, one Oldekop, forbade this on grounds of indecency.

petitions: these would have been in the form of rolled-up scrolls.

75 *(Striking an attitude)*: adopting a pose (here, of a ladykiller).

76   *write some verses for my album*: 'It was fashionable at that time for young ladies to keep albums or autograph books in which they and their friends inscribed verses or songs, mostly of a light romantic kind' (Gogol, 1996, p.187). Oscar Wilde makes fun of this tendency in his play *The Importance of Being Earnest*.

      Shall I compare thee to a summer's day?: first line of Shakespeare's sonnet no. 18. In the original Khlyestakov quotes a couple of lines from an ode by the eighteenth-century poet and scientist Mikhail Lomonosov, familiar to every Russian schoolboy. A sonnet is a verse form of fourteen lines imported into England from Italy during the sixteenth century and then imitated elsewhere.

78   *'Tis but itself the law condemns*: Khlyestakov is quoting from a young man's lament for his beloved borrowed from a poem by N.M. Karamzin, whose main claim to fame is his sentimental novel *Poor Liza* (1792).

80   *give them your blessing*: 'According to Russian custom, a young couple engaged to be married came to the girl's parents, who held up an icon, a crucifix or the right hand and pronounced a blessing on them' (Gogol, 1996, p.285).

      have to get his blessing too, of course: the translators have added this remark of Khlyestakov's in order to explain the excuse, offered on p.89, for his rapid departure. In fact the Mayor and his wife's later explanation is a barefaced untruth, as Khlyestakov says nothing in the original play about obtaining a blessing from his uncle at this point. In any case, he would have needed a blessing from his father, not his uncle.

81   *that dreadful public cart*: the Mayor is surprised that Khlyestakov is using public transport in the form of a springless carriage drawn by relay horses rather than travelling in his own personal carriage.

82   MAYOR. *Aha, Anna . . .*: Act Four having concluded with Khlyestakov's departure, this speech marks the beginning of Act Five in the original.

Decent people!: throughout this speech, the Mayor keeps repeating the word 'kanal'stvo' (a mild oath) and, at one point, refers to the 'iudeiskii narod' ('pack of Jews', rather than 'Judases' as here). Jews were banned from living in central Russia at the time and, as merchants tended to be of non-Russian origin, to call them all 'Jews' was a common form of abuse. An interesting fact about this scene is that 'Maria is silent . . . and is not once spoken to by either parent. Indeed, the Governor never addresses a single word to her throughout the whole play' (Gogol, 1996, p.286).

83   *the red for St Anne, or the blue of the White Eagle*: see note to p.60 on the Order of St Anne. In fact, the Order of St Alexander Nevsky was red and that of St Andrew blue.

84   *they serve coulibiac of salmon*: a whole salmon cooked in pastry.

you counter-jumpers: someone who is so eager to please that he will jump over a counter – an expression applied contemptuously to shopkeepers.

85   *empty a dozen samovars*: a samovar (literally 'a self-boiler') is almost synonymous with the Russian way of life. It is an elaborate urn for storing constant hot water, heated from below by charcoal and with a storage space on top for a teapot which can be constantly replenished with water from a tap in the lower part of the urn.

89   *sneezes*: in folklore, sneezing denotes the presence of the devil.

91   *'Go on, break the seal . . . soon as I touched that wax*: Khlyestakov's letter would not have been placed in an envelope but simply written on a sheet of paper which was then rolled up or folded and sealed with a single blob of wax on the centre of the join.

92   *completely cleaned out*: an idiomatic expression for losing all one's money.

93–4 *'The Schools Superintendent can't speak for twitching'*: in the original, 'The Schools Superintendent absolutely reeks of onions', which may relate to the fact that his name, Luka, is reminiscent of the Russian for onion 'luk').

94 *Ninety-seven, first on the right through the courtyard, third floor*: the details correspond precisely to Gogol's own address in St Petersburg, on Malaya Morskaya Street.
pigs' snouts: in Gogol's collection of short stories, *Evenings on a Farm Near Dikanka*, a connection is made between pigs' snouts and devilish presences.
posting stations: places on a long journey where travellers could rest and hire fresh horses.

96 *Those whom the Gods wish to punish, they first drive mad*: a quotation from the fifth-century BC Greek dramatist Euripides in a later Latin rendition 'Quos Deus vult perdere, prius dementat.'

97 *Enter a* GENDARME *in splendid uniform*: 'The Corps of Gendarmes, a special force of security police commanded by the head of the Third Section, was formed under Nicholas I in 1827. Its officers wore light blue uniforms with epaulettes, white belt, gauntlets and shoulder straps, trousers with footstrap (but not boots), and a plumed helmet' (Gogol, 1996, p.303).
Tableau of consternation: as Gogol pointed out, 'The cast should be specially attentive to the concluding tableau' (see his 'Notes on Characters and Costumes', p.5) and, in the original, he added the following very specific stage directions at the end of the play:

> *The words astound everyone, like thunder. A sound of amazement flies from all the ladies' lips unanimously; the whole group, having suddenly shifted its position, remains petrified.*

THE DUMB SCENE

> *The Mayor is in the middle like a post with outspread arms and his head thrown back. On his right his wife and daughter with their whole bodies straining towards him; behind them the Postmaster, his figure turned into a question mark addressed to the audience; behind him the*

Schools Superintendent bewildered in the most naive way; behind him on the very edge of the stage three ladies, guests, leaning on each other with satirical expressions on their faces, facing directly towards the Mayor's family. On the Mayor's left – Zemlyanika, holding his head somewhat on one side as if listening to something; behind him the Judge with his arms spread wide, moving his lips as if he wanted to whistle or say: 'There you are, Grannie, it's St George's Day again!' [meaning 'Now we've really had it!'] *Behind him, Korobkin, turned to the audience with squinting eyes and a look of caustic reproach at the Mayor; and behind him, on the very edge of the stage, Bobchinsky and Dobchinsky with their hands reaching out towards each other, with mouths agape and eyes popping. The other guests simply stand like posts. For almost a minute and a half the petrified group holds this position before the curtain falls.*

Questions for Further Study

1. What is the significance of the play's epigraph and how might it affect the way in which you read, or perform, *The Government Inspector*?
2. How important a motivating force is fear of the unknown, or that which is 'incognito' in *The Government Inspector*?
3. How significant are the female roles in *The Government Inspector*?
4. How successful is the play in making us aware that the officials are collectively corrupt but, at the same time, corrupt in distinctively individual ways?
5. Consider the significance of the role of Ossip in *The Government Inspector*.
6. How psychologically convincing is Gogol's dramatisation of the encounter between the mayor and Khlyestakov at the inn?
7. Consider the function and importance of minor characters in *The Government Inspector* (i.e. those listed after, and including, the Locksmith's Wife in the cast list).
8. In what ways and to what extent does *The Government Inspector* appear to be concerned with the idea of 'doubleness' or 'duality' in the realm of human affairs?
9. Consider the significance of references to, and consumption of, food and drink in *The Government Inspector*.
10. In what ways and by what means does 'nothing' (a nonentity) become 'something' (a person of consequence) in *The Government Inspector* and what conclusion do you draw from the play as a result?
11. Gogol was a religious moralist much preoccupied with God and the Devil. Does *The Government Inspector*

appear to manifest this concern and, if so, in what ways?

12. Do Gogol's complementary pieces 'On Leaving the Theatre After the Performance of a New Comedy' and 'The Dénouement of *The Government Inspector*' cast any useful light on ways in which the play might be interpreted today?

13. Given that there is a good deal of comic 'business' in the play – funny hats, collapsing doors, exaggerated drunkenness, etc. – is it any wonder that the play is performed farcically or do we need to understand the play's more extreme 'comic' moments in more serious ways?

14. Because *The Government Inspector* describes itself as a comedy, how disturbing do you find the absence of any conventionally 'good' characters or a happy ending?

15. Given that Gogol's requirements are so specific, what are the advantages (or disadvantages) of including (or excluding) the 'dumb scene' at the end of the play?

16. Tsar Nicholas I is reported to have said, after the premiere of *The Government Inspector*, 'Everyone gets it in the neck; including me.' Can we assume that, in spite of the apparent complacency of his response, he got the point? If so, what does this imply about the play's depiction of Tsarist Russia?

17. Consider the implications of Vladimir Nabokov's remark that the play occupies a space between a lightning flash and its succeeding thunderclap.

18. Meyerhold's famous 1926 Soviet production of *The Government Inspector* sought to make the play relevant to the twentieth century. How would you seek to make it relevant to the twenty-first?

19. In Khlyestakov's drunken speech in Act Three, Richard Eyre's production of *The Government Inspector* sought to establish neo-fascist links between a nineteenth-century comedy and twentieth-century history. To what extent do you think the play lends itself to this kind of interpretation?

20. By comparing different English translations of *The Government Inspector*, some of which are described as 'versions' of the play, which do you believe to be the ones which best capture the play's spirit, and why?

Methuen Drama Student Editions

Jean Anouilh *Antigone* • John Arden *Serjeant Musgrave's Dance* • Alan Ayckbourn *Confusions* • Aphra Behn *The Rover* • Edward Bond *Lear* • Bertolt Brecht *The Caucasian Chalk Circle* • *Life of Galileo* • *Mother Courage and her Children* • *The Resistible Rise of Arturo Ui* • *The Threepenny Opera* • Anton Chekhov *The Cherry Orchard* • *The Seagull* • *Three Sisters* • *Uncle Vanya* • Caryl Churchill *Serious Money* • *Top Girls* • Shelagh Delaney *A Taste of Honey* • Euripides *Elektra* • *Medea* • Dario Fo *Accidental Death of an Anarchist* • Michael Frayn *Copenhagen* • John Galsworthy *Strife* • Nikolai Gogol *The Government Inspector* • Robert Holman *Across Oka* • Henrik Ibsen *A Doll's House* • *Hedda Gabler* • Charlotte Keatley *My Mother Said I Never Should* • Bernard Kops *Dreams of Anne Frank* • Federico García Lorca *Blood Wedding* • *The House of Bernarda Alba* (bilingual edition) • *Yerma* (bilingual edition) • David Mamet *Glengarry Glen Ross* • *Oleanna* • Patrick Marber *Closer* • Joe Orton *Loot* • Luigi Pirandello *Six Characters in Search of an Author* • Mark Ravenhill *Shopping and F***ing* • Willy Russell *Blood Brothers* • Sophocles *Antigone* • Wole Soyinka *Death and the King's Horseman* • August Strindberg *Miss Julie* • J. M. Synge *The Playboy of the Western World* • Theatre Workshop *Oh What a Lovely War* • Timberlake Wertenbaker *Our Country's Good* • Arnold Wesker *The Merchant* • Oscar Wilde *The Importance of Being Earnest* • Tennessee Williams *A Streetcar Named Desire* • *The Glass Menagerie*

Methuen Drama World Classics
include

Jean Anouilh (two volumes)
Brendan Behan
Aphra Behn
Bertolt Brecht (eight volumes)
Büchner
Bulgakov
Calderón
Čapek
Anton Chekhov
Noël Coward (eight volumes)
Feydeau (two volumes)
Eduardo De Filippo
Max Frisch
John Galsworthy
Gogol
Gorky (two volumes)
Harley Granville Barker
  (two volumes)
Victor Hugo
Henrik Ibsen (six volumes)
Alfred Jarry
Lorca (three volumes)

Marivaux
Mustapha Matura
David Mercer (two volumes)
Arthur Miller (five volumes)
Molière
Musset
Peter Nichols (two volumes)
Clifford Odets
Joe Orton
A. W. Pinero
Luigi Pirandello
Terence Rattigan
  (two volumes)
W. Somerset Maugham
  (two volumes)
August Strindberg
  (three volumes)
J. M. Synge
Ramón del Valle-Inclán
Frank Wedekind
Oscar Wilde

Methuen Drama Contemporary Dramatists
include

Methuen Drama Classical Greek Dramatists

Aeschylus Plays: One
(Persians, Seven Against Thebes, Suppliants,
Prometheus Bound)

Aeschylus Plays: Two
(Oresteia: Agamemnon, Libation-Bearers, Eumenides)

Aristophanes Plays: One
(Acharnians, Knights, Peace, Lysistrata)

Aristophanes Plays: Two
(Wasps, Clouds, Birds, Festival Time, Frogs)

Aristophanes & Menander: New Comedy
(Women in Power, Wealth, The Malcontent,
The Woman from Samos)

Euripides Plays: One
(Medea, The Phoenician Women, Bacchae)

Euripides Plays: Two
(Hecuba, The Women of Troy, Iphigeneia at Aulis,
Cyclops)

Euripides Plays: Three
(Alkestis, Helen, Ion)

Euripides Plays: Four
(Elektra, Orestes, Iphigeneia in Tauris)

Euripides Plays: Five
(Andromache, Herakles' Children, Herakles)

Euripides Plays: Six
(Hippolytos, Suppliants, Rhesos)

Sophocles Plays: One
(Oedipus the King, Oedipus at Colonus, Antigone)

Sophocles Plays: Two
(Ajax, Women of Trachis, Electra, Philoctetes)